THE FOURTH AMENDMENT

The ★★★★★★★ AMERICAN HERITAGE HISTORY of the BILL of RIGHTS

THE FOURTH AMENDMENT

Paula A. Franklin

Introduction by
WARREN E. BURGER
Chief Justice of the United States
1969–1986

Silver Burdett Press

Cover: Suspects are protected by the Fourth Amendment's rights to be secure against unreasonable searches and seizures.

CONSULTANTS:

Jessie B. Gladden, Divisional Specialist, Office of Social Studies, Baltimore City Schools, Baltimore, Maryland

Michael H. Reggio, Law-Related Education Coordinator, Oklahoma Bar Association, Oklahoma City, Oklahoma

Herbert Sloan, Assistant Professor of History, Barnard College, New York, New York

H. Richard Uviller, Professor of Law, Columbia University School of Law, New York, New York

Text and Cover Design: Circa 86, Inc.

Library of Congress Cataloging-in-Publication Data

Franklin, Paula Angle, 1928-
  The Fourth Amendment/by Paula A. Franklin: with an introduction
by Warren E. Burger
  p. cm.—(The American Heritage history of the Bill of
Rights)
  Includes bibliographical references and indexes.
  Summary: Traces the origins of the Fourth Amendment, which speaks
of citizens' rights in the matter of search and seizure.
  1. United States—Constitutional law—Amendments—4th—History—
Juvenile literature. 2. Searches and seizures—United States—
History—Juvenile literature. 3. {1. United States—Constitutional
law—Amendments—4th—History. 2. Searches and seizures—History.}
I. Title. II. Series.
KF4558 4th. F73 1991
345. 73'0522—dc20
{347.305522}
                                                           90-49863
                                                              CIP
                                                               AC

Manufactured in the United States of America.

ISBN 0-382-24182-7 {lib. bdg.}
10 9 8 7 6 5 4 3 2 1

ISBN 0-382-24195-9 {pbk.}
10 9 8 7 6 5 4 3 2 1

$\mathscr{C}$ONTENTS

WARREN E. BURGER
Chief Justice of the United States, 1969–1986

The Fourth Amendment protects American citizens from unreasonable searches and seizures of their property. Although it is quite specific, its application has been extended to cover modern circumstances the Framers could not have envisioned and the increasing sophistication of law enforcement technology, including aerial searches, wiretapping, and electronic surveillance.

The Fourth Amendment affects every person, not just those involved in court proceedings. It guarantees that Americans can feel safe by preventing any agent of government from searching private property without a good reason authorized by law. The Fourth Amendment does not forbid police to search for or collect evidence that helps prove a crime occurred, or arrest people, so long as the rules for a lawful search are followed. The Framers agreed with the English Lord Justice Edward Coke, who wrote, " A man's house is his castle where even the King may not enter."

Concepts of liberty—the values liberty protects—inspired the Framers of our Constitution and the Bill of Rights to some of their most impassioned eloquence. "Liberty, the greatest of earthly possessions—give us that precious jewel, and you may take everything else," declaimed Patrick Henry. Those toilers in the "vineyard of liberty" sensed the historic nature of their mission, and their foresight accounts for the survival of the Bill of Rights.

The long-term success of the system of ordered liberty set up by our Constitution was by no means foreordained. The bicentennial of the Bill of Rights provides an opportunity to reflect on the significance of the freedoms we enjoy and to commit ourselves to exercise the civic responsibilities required to sustain our constitutional system. The Constitution, including its first ten amendments, the Bill of Rights, has survived two centuries because of its unprecedented philosophical premise: that it derives its power from the people. It is not a grant from the government to the people. In 1787 the masters—the people—were saying to their government—their servant—that certain rights are inherent, natural rights and that they belong to the people, who had those rights before any governments existed. The function of government, they said, was to protect these rights.

The Bill of Rights also owes its continued vitality to the fact that it was drafted by experienced, practical politicians. It was a product of the Framers' essential mistrust of the frailties of human nature. This led them to develop the idea of the separation of powers and to make the Bill of Rights part of the permanent Constitution.

Moreover, the document was designed to be flexible, and the role of providing that flexibility through interpretation has fallen to the judiciary. Indeed, the first commander in chief, George Washington, gave the Supreme Court its moral marching orders two centuries ago when he said, "the administration of justice is the firmest pillar of government." The principle of judicial review as a check on government has perhaps nowhere been more significant than in the protection of individual liberties. It has been my privilege, along with my colleagues on the Court, to ensure the continued vitality of our Bill of Rights. As John Marshall asked, long before he became chief justice, "To what quarter will you look for a protection from an infringement on the Constitution, if you will not give the power to the judiciary?"

But the preservation of the Bill of Rights is not the sole responsibility of the judiciary. Rather, judges, legislatures, and presidents are partners with every American; liberty is the responsibility of every public officer and every citizen. In this spirit all Americans should become acquainted with the principles and history of this most remarkable document. Its bicentennial should not be simply a celebration but the beginning of an ongoing process. Americans must—by their conduct—guarantee that it continues to protect the sacred rights of our uniquely multicultural population. We must not fail to exercise our rights to vote, to participate in government and community activities, and to implement the principles of liberty, tolerance, opportunity, and justice for all.

T H E A M E R I C A N H E R I T A G E
HISTORY OF THE BILL OF RIGHTS

THE FIRST AMENDMENT
by Philip A. Klinkner

THE SECOND AMENDMENT
by Joan C. Hawxhurst

THE THIRD AMENDMENT
by Burnham Holmes

THE FOURTH AMENDMENT
by Paula A. Franklin

THE FIFTH AMENDMENT
by Burnham Holmes

THE SIXTH AMENDMENT
by Eden Force

THE SEVENTH AMENDMENT
by Lila E. Summer

THE EIGHTH AMENDMENT
by Vincent Buranelli

THE NINTH AMENDMENT
by Philip A. Klinkner

THE TENTH AMENDMENT
by Judith Adams

The Bill of Rights

AMENDMENT 1*

Article Congress shall make no law respecting an establishment of religion, or prohibiting the free exercise thereof; or abridging the freedom of speech, or of the press; or the right of the people peaceably to assemble, and to petition the Government for a redress of grievances.

AMENDMENT 2

Article A well regulated Militia, being necessary to the security of a free State, the right of the people to keep and bear Arms, shall not be infringed.

AMENDMENT 3

Article No Soldier shall, in time of peace be quartered in any house, without the consent of the Owner, nor in time of war, but in a manner to be prescribed by law.

AMENDMENT 4

Article The right of the people to be secure in their persons, houses, papers, and effects, against unreasonable searches and seizures, shall not be violated, and no Warrants shall issue, but upon probable cause, supported by Oath or affirmation, and particularly describing the place to be searched, and the persons or things to be seized.

AMENDMENT 5

Article No person shall be held to answer for a capital, or otherwise infamous crime, unless on a presentment or indictment of a Grand Jury, except in cases arising in the land or naval forces, or in the Militia, when in actual service in time of War or public danger; nor shall any person be subject for the same offence to be twice put in jeopardy of life or limb; nor shall be compelled in any criminal case to be a witness against himself, nor be deprived of life, liberty, or property, without due process of law; nor shall private property be taken for public use without just compensation.

AMENDMENT 6

Article In all criminal prosecutions, the accused shall enjoy the right to a speedy and public trial, by an impartial jury of the State and district wherein the crime shall have been committed, which district shall have been previously ascertained by law, and to be informed of the nature and cause of the accusation; to be confronted with the witnesses against him; to have compulsory process for obtaining Witnesses in his favor, and to have the assistance of counsel for his defence.

AMENDMENT 7

Article In Suits at common law, where the value in controversy shall exceed twenty dollars, the right of trial by jury shall be preserved, and no fact tried by a jury, shall be otherwise reexamined in any Court of the United States, than according to the rules of the common law.

AMENDMENT 8

Article Excessive bail shall not be required, nor excessive fines imposed, nor cruel and unusual punishments inflicted.

AMENDMENT 9

Article The enumeration in the Constitution, of certain rights, shall not be construed to deny or disparage others retained by the people.

AMENDMENT 10

Article The powers not delegated to the United States by the Constitution, nor prohibited by it to the States, are reserved to the States respectively, or to the people.

*Note that each of the first ten amendments to the original Constitution is called an "Article." None of these amendments had actual numbers at the time of their ratification.

TIME CHART

THE HISTORY OF THE
BILL OF RIGHTS

1770s–1790s

1774 Quartering Act
1775 Revolutionary War begins
1776 Declaration of Independence is signed.
1783 Revolutionary War ends.
1787 Constitutional Convention writes the U.S. Constitution.
1788 U.S. Constitution is ratified by most states.
1789 Congress proposes the Bill of Rights
1791 The Bill of Rights is ratified by the states.
1792 Militia Act

1800s–1820s

1803 *Marbury* v. *Madison.* Supreme Court declares that it has the power of judicial review and exercises it. This is the first case in which the Court holds a law of Congress unconstitutional.
1807 Trial of Aaron Burr. Ruling that juries may have knowledge of a case so long as they have not yet formed an opinion.
1813 Kentucky becomes the first state to outlaw concealed weapons.
1824 *Gibbons* v. *Ogden.* Supreme Court defines Congress's power to regulate commerce, including trade between states and within states if that commerce affects other states.

1830s–1870s

1833 *Barron* v. *Baltimore.* Supreme Court rules that Bill of Rights applies only to actions of the federal government, not to the states and local governments.

1851 *Cooley* v. *Board of Wardens of the Port of Philadelphia.* Supreme Court rules that states can apply their own rules to some foreign and interstate commerce if their rules are of a local nature—unless or until Congress makes rules for particular situations.

1857 *Dred Scott* v. *Sandford.* Supreme Court denies that African Americans are citizens even if they happen to live in a "free state."

1862 Militia Act

1865 Thirteenth Amendment is ratified. Slavery is not allowed in the United States.

1868 Fourteenth Amendment is ratified. All people born or naturalized in the United States are citizens. Their privileges and immunities are protected, as are their life, liberty, and property according to due process. They have equal protection of the laws.

1873 *Slaughterhouse* cases. Supreme Court rules that the Fourteenth Amendment does not limit state power to make laws dealing with economic matters. Court mentions the unenumerated right to political participation.

1876 *United States* v. *Cruikshank.* Supreme Court rules that the right to bear arms for a lawful purpose is not an absolute right granted by the Constitution. States can limit this right and make their own gun-control laws.

1880s–1920s

1884 *Hurtado* v. *California.* Supreme Court rules that the right to a grand jury indictment doesn't apply to the states.

1896 *Plessy* v. *Ferguson.* Supreme Court upholds a state law based on "separate but equal" facilities for different races.

1903 Militia Act creates National Guard.

1905 *Lochner* v. *New York.* Supreme Court strikes down a state law regulating maximum work hours.

1914 *Weeks* v. *United States.* Supreme Court establishes that illegally obtained evidence, obtained by unreasonable search and seizure, cannot be used in federal trials.

1918 *Hammer* v. *Dagenhart.* Supreme Court declares unconstitutional a federal law prohibiting the shipment between states of goods made by young children.

1923 *Meyer* v. *Nebraska.* Supreme Court rules that a law banning teaching of foreign languages or teaching in languages other than English is unconstitutional. Court says that certain areas of people's private lives are protected from government interference.

1925 *Carroll* v. *United States.* Supreme Court allows searches of automobiles without a search warrant under some circumstances.

1925 *Gitlow* v. *New York.* Supreme Court rules that freedom of speech and freedom of the press are protected from state actions by the Fourteenth Amendment.

1930s

1931 *Near* v. *Minnesota*. Supreme Court rules that liberty of the press and of speech are safeguarded from state action.

1931 *Stromberg* v. *California*. Supreme Court extends concept of freedom of speech to symbolic actions such as displaying a flag.

1932 *Powell* v. *Alabama* (*First Scottsboro* case). Supreme Court rules that poor defendants have a right to an appointed lawyer when tried for crimes that may result in the death penalty.

1934 National Firearms Act becomes the first federal law to restrict the keeping and bearing of arms.

1935 *Norris* v. *Alabama* (*Second Scottsboro* case). Supreme Court reverses the conviction of an African American because of the long continued excluding of African Americans from jury service in the trial area.

1937 *Palko* v. *Connecticut*. Supreme Court refuses to require states to protect people under the double jeopardy clause of the Bill of Rights. But the case leads to future application of individual rights in the Bill of Rights to the states on a case-by-case basis.

1937 *DeJonge* v. *Oregon*. Supreme Court rules that freedom of assembly and petition are protected against state laws.

1939 *United States* v. *Miller*. Supreme Court rules that National Firearms Act of 1934 does not violate Second Amendment.

1940s–1950s

1940 *Cantwell* v. *Connecticut*. Supreme Court rules that free exercise of religion is protected against state laws.

1943 *Barnette* v. *West Virginia State Board of Education*. Supreme Court rules that flag salute laws are unconstitutional.

1946 *Theil* v. *Pacific Railroad*. Juries must be a cross section of the community, excluding no group based on religion, race, sex, or economic status.

1947 *Everson* v. *Board of Education*. Supreme Court rules that government attempts to impose religious practices, the establishment of religion, is forbidden to the states.

1948 *In re Oliver*. Supreme Court rules that defendants have a right to public trial in nonfederal trials.

1949 *Wolf* v. *California*. Supreme Court rules that freedom from unreasonable searches and seizures also applies to states.

1954 *Brown* v. *Board of Education of Topeka*. Supreme Court holds that segregation on the basis of race (in public education) denies equal protection of the laws.

1958 *NAACP* v. *Alabama*. Supreme Court rules that the privacy of membership lists in an organization is part of the right to freedom of assembly and association.

1961 *Mapp* v. *Ohio.* Supreme Court rules that illegally obtained evidence must not be allowed in state criminal trials.

1962 *Engel* v. *Vitale.* Supreme Court strikes down state-sponsored school prayer, saying it is no business of government to compose official prayers as part of a religious program carried on by the government.

1963 *Gideon* v. *Wainwright.* Supreme Court rules that the right of people accused of serious crimes to be represented by an appointed counsel applies to state criminal trials.

1964 Civil Rights Act is passed.

1964 *Malloy* v. *Hogan.* Supreme Court rules that the right to protection against forced self-incrimination applies to state trials.

1965 *Griswold* v. *Connecticut.* Supreme Court rules that there is a right to privacy in marriage and declares unconstitutional a state law banning the use of or the giving of information about birth control.

1965 *Pointer* v. *Texas.* Supreme Court rules that the right to confront witnesses against an accused person applies to state trials.

1966 *Parker* v. *Gladden.* Supreme Court ruling is interpreted to mean that the right to an impartial jury is applied to the states.

1966 *Miranda* v. *Arizona.* Supreme Court extends the protection against forced self-incrimination. Police have to inform people in custody of their rights before questioning them.

1967 *Katz* v. *United States.* Supreme Court rules that people's right to be free of unreasonable searches includes protection against electronic surveillance.

1967 *Washington* v. *Texas.* Supreme Court rules that accused people have the right to have witnesses in their favor brought into court.

1967 *In re Gault.* Supreme Court rules that juvenile proceedings that might lead to the young person's being sent to a state institution must follow due process and fair treatment. These include the rights against forced self-incrimination, to counsel, to confront witnesses.

1967 *Klopfer* v. *North Carolina.* Supreme Court rules that the right to a speedy trial applies to state trials.

1968 *Duncan* v. *Louisiana.* Supreme Court rules that the right to a jury trial in criminal cases applies to state trials.

1969 *Benton* v. *Maryland.* Supreme Court rules that the protection against double jeopardy applies to the states.

1969 *Brandenburg* v. *Ohio.* Supreme Court rules that speech calling for the use of force or crime can only be prohibited if it is directed to bringing about immediate lawless action and is likely to bring about such action.

1970 *Williams* v. *Florida.* Juries in cases that do not lead to the possibility of the death penalty may consist of six jurors rather than twelve.

1971 *Pentagon Papers* case. Freedom of the press is protected by forbidding prior restraint.

1971 *Duke Power Co.* v. *Carolina Environmental Study Group, Inc.* Supreme Court upholds state law limiting liability of federally licensed power companies in the event of a nuclear accident.

1972 *Furman* v. *Georgia.* Supreme Court rules that the death penalty (as it was then decided upon) is cruel and unusual punishment and therefore unconstitutional.

1972 *Argersinger* v. *Hamlin.* Supreme Court rules that right to counsel applies to all criminal cases that might involve a jail term.

1973 *Roe* v. *Wade.* Supreme Court declares that the right to privacy protects a woman's right to end pregnancy by abortion under specified circumstances.

1976 *Gregg* v. *Georgia.* Supreme Court rules that the death penalty is to be allowed if it is decided upon in a consistent and reasonable way, if the sentencing follows strict guidelines, and if the penalty is not required for certain crimes.

1976 *National League of Cities* v. *Usery.* Supreme Court holds that the Tenth Amendment prevents Congress from making federal minimum wage and overtime rules apply to state and city workers.

1981 *Quilici* v. *Village of Morton Grove.* U.S. district court upholds a local ban on sale and possession of handguns.

1985 *Garcia* v. *San Antonio Metropolitan Transit Authority.* Supreme Court rules that Congress can make laws dealing with wages and hour rules applied to city-owned transportation systems.

1989 *Webster* v. *Reproductive Health Services.* Supreme Court holds that a state may prohibit all use of public facilities and publicly employed staff in abortions.

1989 *Johnson* v. *Texas.* Supreme Court rules that flag burning is protected and is a form of "symbolic speech."

1990 *Cruzan* v. *Missouri Department of Health.* Supreme Court recognizes for the first time a very sick person's right to die without being forced to undergo unwanted medical treatment and a person's right to a living will.

1990 *Noriega–CNN* case. Supreme Court upholds lower federal court's decision to allow temporary prior restraint thus limiting the First Amendment right of freedom of the press.

The Birth of the Bill of Rights

"We hold these truths to be self-evident, that all men are created equal,
that they are endowed by their Creator with certain unalienable Rights,
that among these are Life, Liberty, and the pursuit of Happiness."

THE DECLARATION OF INDEPENDENCE (1776)

A brave Chinese student standing in front of a line of tanks,
Eastern Europeans marching against the secret police, happy
crowds dancing on top of the Berlin Wall—these were recent scenes
of people trying to gain their freedom or celebrating it. The scenes
and the events that sparked them will live on in history. They also
show the lasting gift that is our Bill of Rights. The freedoms
guaranteed by the Bill of Rights have guided and inspired millions
of people all over the world in their struggle for freedom.

The Colonies Gain Their Freedom

Like many countries today, the United States fought to gain
freedom and democracy for itself. The American colonies had a
revolution from 1775 to 1783 to free themselves from British rule.

The colonists fought to free themselves because they believed
that the British had violated, or gone against, their rights. The
colonists held what some considered the extreme idea that all

James Madison is known as both the "Father of the Constitution" and the
"Father of the Bill of Rights." In 1789 he proposed to Congress the
amendments that became the Bill of Rights. Madison served two terms as
president of the United States from 1809 to 1817.

The Raising of the Liberty Pole by John McRae. In 1776, American colonists hoisted liberty poles as symbols of liberty and freedom from British rule. At the top they usually placed a liberty cap. Such caps resembled the caps given to slaves in ancient Rome when they were freed.

persons are born with certain rights. They believed that these rights could not be taken away, even by the government. The importance our nation gave to individual rights can be seen in the Declaration of Independence. The Declaration, written by Thomas Jefferson in 1776, states:

> We hold these truths to be self-evident, that all men are created equal, that they are endowed by their Creator with certain unaliena-ble Rights, that among these are Life, Liberty, and the pursuit of Happiness.

The United States won its independence from Britain in 1783. But with freedom came the difficult job of forming a government. The Americans wanted a government that was strong enough to keep peace and prosperity, but not so strong that it might take away the rights for which the Revolution had been fought. The Articles of Confederation was the country's first written plan of government.

The Articles of Confederation, becoming law in 1781, created a weak national government. The defects in the Articles soon became clear to many Americans. Because the United States did not have a strong national government, its economy suffered. Under the Articles, Congress did not have the power to tax. It had to ask the states for money or borrow it. There was no separate president or court system. Nine of the states had to agree before Congress's bills became law. In 1786 economic problems caused farmers in Massachusetts to revolt. The national government was almost powerless to stop the revolt. It was also unable to build an army or navy strong enough to protect the United States's borders and its ships on the high seas.

The Constitution Is Drawn Up

The nation's problems had to be solved. So, in February 1787, the Continental Congress asked the states to send delegates to a convention to discuss ways of improving the Articles. That May, fifty-five delegates, from every state except Rhode Island, met in Philadelphia. The group included some of the country's most famous leaders: George Washington, hero of the Revolution; Benjamin Franklin, publisher, inventor, and diplomat; and James Madison, a leading critic of the Articles. Madison would soon become the guiding force behind the Constitutional Convention.

After a long, hot summer of debate the delegates finally drew up the document that became the U.S. Constitution. It set up a strong central government. But it also divided power between three branches of the federal government. These three branches were the executive branch (the presidency), the legislative branch (Congress), and the judicial branch (the courts). Each was given one part of the government's power. This division was to make sure that no single branch became so powerful that it could violate the people's rights.

The legislative branch (made up of the House of Representatives and the Senate) would have the power to pass laws, raise taxes and spend money, regulate the national economy, and declare war. The executive branch was given the power to carry out the laws, run foreign affairs, and command the military.

The Signing of the Constitution painted by Thomas Rossiter. The Constitutional Convention met in Philadelphia from May into September 1787. The proposed Constitution contained protection for some individual rights such as protection against *ex post facto* laws and bills of attainder. When the Constitution was ratified by the required number of states in 1788, however, it did not have a bill of rights.

The role of the judicial branch in this plan was less clear. The Constitution said that the judicial branch would have "judicial power." However, it was unclear exactly what this power was. Over the years "judicial power" has come to mean "judicial review." The power of judicial review allows the federal courts to reject laws passed by Congress or the state legislatures that they believe violate the Constitution.

Judicial review helps protect our rights. It allows federal courts to reject laws that violate the Constitution's guarantees of individual rights. Because of this power, James Madison believed that the courts would be an "impenetrable bulwark," an unbreakable wall, against any attempt by government to take away these rights.

The Constitution did more than divide the power of the federal government among the three branches. It also divided power between the states and the federal government. This division of power is known as *federalism*. Federalism means that the federal

government has control over certain areas. These include regulating the national economy and running foreign and military affairs. The states have control over most other areas. For example, they regulate their economies and make most other laws. Once again, the Framers (writers) of the Constitution hoped that the division of powers would keep both the states and the federal government from becoming too strong and possibly violating individual rights.

The new Constitution did *not,* however, contain a bill of rights. Such a bill would list the people's rights and would forbid the government from interfering with them. The only discussion of the topic came late in the convention. At that time, George Mason of Virginia called for a bill of rights. A Connecticut delegate, Roger Sherman, disagreed. He claimed that a bill of rights was not needed. In his view, the Constitution did not take away any of the rights in the bills of rights in the state constitutions. These had been put in place during the Revolution. The other delegates agreed with Roger Sherman. Mason's proposal was voted down by all.

Yet the Constitution was not without guarantees of individual rights. One of these rights was the protection of *habeas corpus.* This is a legal term that refers to the right of someone who has been arrested to be brought into court and formally charged with a crime. Another right forbade *ex post facto* laws. These are laws that outlaw actions that took place before the passage of the laws. Other parts of the Constitution forbade bills of attainder (laws pronouncing a person guilty of a crime without trial), required jury trials, restricted convictions for treason, and guaranteed a republican form of government. That is a government in which political power rests with citizens who vote for elected officials and representatives responsible to the voters. The Constitution also forbade making public officials pass any "religious test." This meant that religious requirements could not be forced on public officials.

The Debate Over the New Constitution

Once it was written, the Constitution had to be ratified, or approved, by nine of the states before it could go into effect. The new

Constitution created much controversy. Heated battles raged in many states over whether or not to approve the document. One of the main arguments used by those who opposed the Constitution (the Anti-Federalists) was that the Constitution made the federal government too strong. They feared that it might violate the rights of the people just as the British government had. Although he had helped write the Constitution, Anti-Federalist George Mason opposed it for this reason. He claimed that he would sooner chop off his right hand than put it to the Constitution as it then stood.

To correct what they viewed as flaws in the Constitution, the Anti-Federalists insisted that it have a bill of rights. The fiery orator of the Revolution, Patrick Henry, another Anti-Federalist, exclaimed, "Liberty, the greatest of all earthly blessings—give us that precious jewel, and you may take every thing else!"

Although he was not an Anti-Federalist, Thomas Jefferson also believed that a bill of rights was needed. He wrote a letter to James Madison, a wavering Federalist, in which he said: "A bill of rights is what the people are entitled to against every government on earth."

Supporters of the Constitution (the Federalists) argued that it did not need a bill of rights. One reason they stated, similar to that given at the Philadelphia convention, was that most state constitutions had a bill of rights. Nothing in the Constitution would limit or abolish these rights. In 1788 James Madison wrote that he thought a bill of rights would provide only weak "parchment barriers" against attempts by government to take away individual rights. He believed that history had shown that a bill of rights was ineffective on "those occasions when its control [was] needed most."

The views of the Anti-Federalists seem to have had more support than did those of the Federalists. The Federalists came to realize that without a bill of rights, the states might not approve the new Constitution. To ensure ratification, the Federalists therefore agreed to support adding a bill of rights to the Constitution.

With this compromise, eleven of the thirteen states ratified the Constitution by July 1788. The new government of the United States was born. The two remaining states, North Carolina and

Rhode Island, in time accepted the new Constitution. North Carolina approved it in November 1789 and Rhode Island in May 1790.

James Madison Calls for a Bill of Rights

On April 30, 1789, George Washington took the oath of office as president. The new government was launched. One of its first jobs was to amend, or change, the Constitution to include a bill of rights. This is what many of the states had called for during the ratification process. Leading this effort in the new Congress was James Madison. He was a strong supporter of individual rights. As a member of the Virginia legislature, he had helped frame the Virginia Declaration of Rights. He had also fought for religious liberty.

Madison, however, had at first opposed including a bill of rights. But his views had changed. He feared that the Constitution would not be ratified by enough states to become law unless the Federalists offered to include a bill of rights. Madison also knew that many people were afraid of the new government. He feared they might oppose its actions or attempt to undo it. He said a bill of rights "will kill the opposition everywhere, and by putting an end to disaffection to [discontent with] the Government itself, enable the administration to venture on measures not otherwise safe."

On June 8, 1789, the thirty-eight-year-old Madison rose to speak in the House of Representatives. He called for several changes to the Constitution that contained the basis of our present Bill of Rights. Despite his powerful words, Madison's speech did not excite his listeners. Most Federalists in Congress opposed a bill of rights. Others believed that the new Constitution should be given more time to operate before Congress considered making any changes. Many Anti-Federalists wanted a new constitutional convention. There, they hoped to greatly limit the powers of the federal government. These Anti-Federalists thought that adding a bill of rights to the Constitution would prevent their movement for a new convention.

Finally, in August, Madison persuaded the House to consider

his amendments. The House accepted most of them. However, instead of being placed in the relevant sections of the Constitution, as Madison had called for, the House voted to add them as separate amendments. This change—listing the amendments together—made the Bill of Rights the distinct document that it is today.

After approval by the House, the amendments went to the Senate. The Senate dropped what Madison considered the most important part of his plan. This was the protection of freedom of the press, freedom of religious belief, and the right to trial by jury from violation by the states. Protection of these rights from violation by state governments would have to wait until after the Fourteenth Amendment was adopted in 1868.

The House and the Senate at last agreed on ten amendments to protect individual rights. What rights were protected? Here is a partial list:

The First Amendment protects freedom of religion, of speech, of the press, of peaceful assembly, and of petition.

The Second Amendment gives to the states the right to keep a militia (a volunteer, reserve military force) and to the people the right to keep and bear arms.

The Third Amendment prevents the government from keeping troops in private homes during wartime.

The Fourth Amendment protects individuals from unreasonable searches and seizures by the government.

The Fifth Amendment states that the government must get an indictment (an official ruling that a crime has been committed) before someone can be tried for a serious crime. This amendment bans "double jeopardy." This means trying a person twice for the same criminal offense. It also protects people from having to testify against themselves in court.

The Fifth Amendment also says that the government cannot take away a person's "life, liberty, or property, without due process of law." This means that the government must follow fair and just procedures if it takes away a person's "life, liberty, or property." Finally, the Fifth Amendment says that if the government takes property from an individual for public use, it must pay that person an adequate sum of money for the property.

The Sixth Amendment requires that all criminal trials be speedy and public, and decided by a fair jury. The amendment also allows people on trial to know what offense they have been charged with. It also allows them to be present when others testify against them, to call witnesses to their defense, and to have the help of a lawyer.

The Seventh Amendment provides for a jury trial in all cases involving amounts over $20.

The Eighth Amendment forbids unreasonably high bail (money paid to free someone from jail before his or her trial), unreasonably large fines, and cruel and unusual punishments.

The Ninth Amendment says that the rights of the people are not limited only to those listed in the Bill of Rights.

Finally, the Tenth Amendment helps to establish federalism by giving to the states and the people any powers not given to the federal government by the Constitution.

After being approved by the House and the Senate, the amendments were sent to the states for adoption in October 1789. By December 1791, three-fourths of the states had approved the ten amendments we now know as the Bill of Rights. The Bill of Rights had become part of the U.S. Constitution.

How Our Court System Works

Many of the events in this book concern court cases involving the Bill of Rights. To help understand how the U.S. court system works, here is a brief description.

The U.S. federal court system has three levels. At the lowest level are the federal district courts. There are ninety-four district courts, each covering a different area of the United States and its territories. Most cases having to do with the Constitution begin in the district courts.

People who lose their cases in the district courts may then appeal to the next level in the court system, the federal courts of appeals. To appeal means to take your case to a higher court in an attempt to change the lower court's decision. Here, those who are making the appeal try to obtain a different judgment. There are thirteen federal courts of appeals in the United States.

People who lose in the federal courts of appeals may then take their case to the U.S. Supreme Court. It is the highest court in the land. The Supreme Court has the final say in a case. You cannot appeal a Supreme Court decision.

The size of the Supreme Court is set by Congress and has changed over the years. Since 1869 the Supreme Court has been made up of nine justices. One is the chief justice of the United States, and eight are associate justices. The justices are named by the president and confirmed by the Senate.

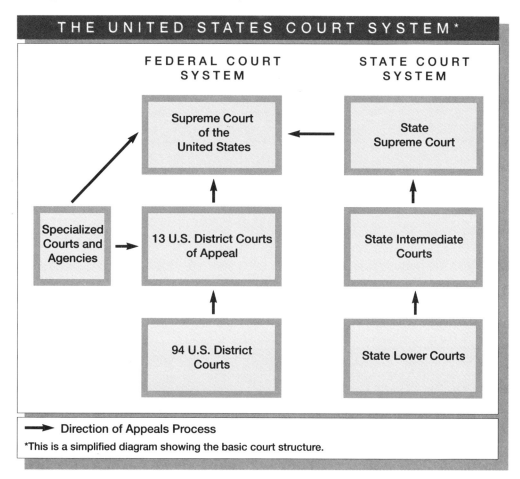

THE UNITED STATES COURT SYSTEM*

FEDERAL COURT SYSTEM

STATE COURT SYSTEM

Supreme Court of the United States

State Supreme Court

Specialized Courts and Agencies

13 U.S. District Courts of Appeal

State Intermediate Courts

94 U.S. District Courts

State Lower Courts

➤ Direction of Appeals Process

*This is a simplified diagram showing the basic court structure.

In the Supreme Court, a simple majority of votes is needed to decide a case. If there is a tie, the lower court's decision remains in effect. When the chief justice votes on the majority side, he or she can assign the writing of the opinion to any of the majority justices, including himself or herself. The opinion states the Court's decision and the reasons for it. Who writes the opinion when the chief justice hasn't voted on the majority side? In that case, the longest-serving associate justice who voted for the majority decision can assign the writing to any of the majority justices, including himself or herself.

What if a justice has voted for the majority decision but doesn't agree with the reasons given in the majority opinion? He or she may write what is called a concurring opinion. That is one which agrees with the Court's decision but for different reasons.

Those justices who disagree with the Court's decision may write what is called a dissenting opinion. They have the opportunity to explain why they think the majority Supreme Court decision is wrong.

In addition to the federal court system, each state has its own system of courts. These systems vary from state to state. However, they are usually made up of two or three levels of lower courts and then the state's highest court, usually called the state supreme court. Those who lose their cases in the state supreme court may appeal those decisions to the federal court system, usually to the Supreme Court.

Not all cases that are appealed to the Supreme Court are heard by it. In fact, very few of them are. For the Supreme Court to decide to hear a case, four of the nine justices must vote to hear it. If fewer than four justices vote to hear the case, then the judgment of the lower court remains in effect.

The Fourth Amendment

The Fourth Amendment protects Americans against "unreasonable" searches and seizures of themselves, their houses, and the things they own. It also provides guidelines for issuing warrants, the documents that allow the police to conduct searches and seizures. The Fourth Amendment grew out of wrongs the colonists suffered during British rule. In the 200 years since it was added to the Constitution of the United States, its protections have been applied in situations the Framers could never have imagined, from highway roadblocks to electronic surveillance. The far-reaching applications of the Fourth Amendment make it one of the most vital guarantees of the Bill of Rights.

PHILIP A. KLINKNER

CHAPTER 1

How the Fourth Amendment Came to Be

"The house of every one is to him as his castle and fortress, as well for his defence against injury and violence as for his repose."

SIR EDWARD COKE, in *Semayne's Case* (1604)

Daniel Malcom, a rich colonial merchant, lived in a fine house in Boston. One September day in 1766, a fellow Bostonian, Ebenezer Richardson, reported Malcom to the customs office. The customs office enforced rules about imports and exports—that is, goods shipped into or out of the American colonies. According to Richardson, Malcom had stored in his cellar large amounts of imported wine and brandy on which he had paid no taxes. Many colonists did this. But it was against the law.

On September 24, a Wednesday morning, customs officials went to Malcom's house. They took with them a writ of assistance. This document was a kind of search warrant. It allowed colonial officials to search people's homes or businesses freely. The inspectors did not have to specify the place they were searching or what they were looking for. In addition, the writ was good for an almost unlimited time (during daylight hours). This meant that officials could search whenever they wanted to over a period of days, weeks, or months.

A customs official in Boston being tarred and feathered. This illustration appeared in a London paper in 1774. It was meant to show the cruelty of colonists who refused to pay the customs, or taxes, on imported goods.

When the officials asked to inspect Malcom's house, he showed them everything but one cellar room. That, he said, was rented to someone else and the inspectors had no right to look at it. An argument followed: In the words of one of the officials, Malcom said:

> [H]e knew the Laws of England and Ireland, and That Nobody had a Right to come and search his House, neither should they; and if they attempted it, he would blow their Brains out.

What to do next? The officials left Malcom's house and returned a few hours later with the sheriff. By this time a crowd had gathered. The people made it clear, as the official put it,

> that we and the other Officers had better get away before any mischief was done, for if the Officers attempted to force the House or Cellar they would be Insulted and Ill used and there would be Blood shed.

Paul Revere, who was among the crowd of onlookers, later reported that the chief customs official "looked very angry." And well he might. There was nothing he could do. Finally, he gave up, abandoned the search, and never returned. Malcom's house, and his cellar, were safe from outsiders.

An Unpopular Practice

England had begun making settlements along the Atlantic coast of North America during the early 1600s. Thousands of Europeans crossed the ocean to live in the English colonies. The newcomers were attracted by the freedom and opportunity the new land offered. (It is well to remember, however, that some groups did not share in these benefits. One group, the Native Americans, was either defeated or moved west. Another group, blacks from Africa, was enslaved.)

For many years, relations between the colonies and England were good. The colonists felt that most of the English laws and traditions that governed them were fair. There were indeed many trade regulations, or laws, limiting exports and imports. But these rules were not strictly enforced. For example, the colonists were able to smuggle in a lot of goods without paying the necessary taxes on them.

The situation changed during the mid-1700s, however. England decided to enforce its trade laws. It needed money to pay for wars it was waging against France. This is how the writs of assistance came to be used. A writ of assistance enabled customs officials to search for smuggled goods wherever they wanted to do so. If necessary, they could ask for help from anyone in the area. (That is why these warrants were called writs of assistance.)

Hardly anybody liked the writs of assistance. The English had long believed that "a man's home is his castle." But in England itself, so-called general warrants—similar to writs of assistance—had been in use since the 1500s. Most commonly, searches of private premises were carried out in order to enforce official censorship. (Premises are buildings or parts of buildings and the land around them.) The Crown, or government, controlled the press by giving only certain printers licenses and examining works before they were printed. If the authorities suspected someone of running an unlicensed printshop, they used a general warrant to search the premises and seize illegal goods.

General warrants were also used to enforce tax laws. For example, manufacturers were supposed to pay taxes on certain alcoholic beverages. A general warrant would authorize the search of premises if the owner was believed to be making or selling goods that had not been taxed.

There were many protests against general warrants. Most of them came from experts in common law. (Common law has developed in England and the United States through judicial, or court, decisions rather than through a series of laws.) Sir Edward Coke (pronounced COOK), a famous English judge, stated that common law gave no power "to break open any man's house to search for a felon or stolen goods either in the day or night." During the late 1600s, Parliament, the English lawmaking body, did away with one tax because of general warrants. Political leaders said that the searches required to enforce the tax were "a badge of slavery upon the whole people, exposing every man's house to be entered into, and searched by persons unknown to him." When the Cider Act of 1763 required the use of a general warrant, statesman William Pitt thundered:

> The poorest man may in his cottage bid defiance to all the force of the Crown. It may be frail—its roof may shake—the wind may blow through it—the storm may enter—the rain may enter—but the King of England cannot enter: all his force dares not cross the threshold of that ruined tenement [dwelling]!

Some general warrants were declared illegal in England in 1766. But they were not completely abolished until the 1780s.

England's colonists in North America thought writs of assistance were especially unjust. Many Americans were becoming impatient with English rule. These Patriots, as they were called, saw the writs as weapons England used to dominate the colonies from afar. In fact, the writs were the subject of a famous speech made just a few years before the Malcom affair.

Bostonians Speak Out

In 1761, a group of Boston merchants requested that writs of assistance be abolished. Speaking for them was a Patriot named James Otis. He had been the king's chief lawyer in Boston. But he became so angry about the writs that he resigned his position. Otis attacked writs of assistance in a fiery speech given before the Massachusetts authorities. Here is some of what he said:

I take this opportunity to declare that . . . I will to my dying day oppose with all the powers and faculties [abilities] God has given me, all such instruments of slavery on the one hand, and villainy on the other, as this writ of assistance is. It appears to me the worst instrument of arbitrary [unlimited] power, the most destructive of English liberty and the fundamental principles of law, that ever was found in an English law-book. . . . One of the most essential branches of English liberty is the freedom of one's house. A man's

James Otis of Massachusetts being cheered after protesting against writs of assistance at the Boston Town House in 1761. He said that one "of the most essential branches of English liberty is the freedom of one's house. A man's house is his castle."

house is his castle. This writ, if it should be declared legal, would totally annihilate [wipe out] this privilege. Custom-house officers may enter our houses when they please; we are commanded to permit their entry. Their menial [lowly] servants may enter, may break locks, bars, and everything in their way; and whether they break through malice [spite] or revenge, no man, no court, can inquire.

One of those present when Otis made this speech was John Adams, who would become a leader of the American Revolution and, later, president of the United States. Adams wrote about Otis years later:

He was a flame of fire! . . . Every man of a crowded audience appeared to me to go away, as I did, ready to take arms against writs of assistance. . . . Then and there the Child Independence was born. In fifteen years, namely in 1776, he grew up to manhood, and declared himself free.

At the time, however, the authorities did not agree with Otis. They continued to issue writs of assistance. And the colonists continued to complain. A Boston report of 1772 was typically outspoken. Because of writs of assistance, it said,

Officers . . . break thro' the sacred rights of the *Domicil* [home], ransack men's houses, destroy their securities, carry off their property, and . . . commit the most horred [horrid] murders.

Independence and After

Writs of assistance were an important reason "the Child Independence" came into being with the Declaration of Independence in 1776. But freedom had to be fought for. This struggle, the American Revolution, lasted until 1783. During this time, almost all of the states—the former colonies—drew up constitutions. Eight state constitutions had a bill of rights. Most state bills of rights guaranteed that citizens could practice their religion without interference and, if accused of wrongdoing, be tried by a jury. All of the bills of rights protected citizens from writs of assistance by outlawing unreasonable searches and seizures.

After the United States won its freedom from Britain in 1783, it was governed according to the Articles of Confederation. This document included no bill of rights. Many leaders thought that citizens would be well protected by the constitutions of their own states.

Anger over what American colonists regarded as arbitrary British rule grew in the 1760s and 1770s. Fighting broke out in 1775.

The New Constitution

As the Foreword to this book states, the Articles of Confederation was replaced by our present Constitution in 1789. Many states agreed to ratify the new document only if a bill of rights was added to it. Provisions for a bill of rights were offered at several of the state ratifying conventions. Pennsylvania, for instance, suggested fourteen such provisions. One of them prohibited "warrants unsupported by evidence or seizure of persons or property not particularly described." Massachusetts had a similar provision. Virginia declared that "every freeman has a right to be secure against unreasonable searches and seizures and general warrants ought not to be granted."

James Madison was given the task of preparing a bill of rights. The list he presented to Congress included this provision:

> The rights of the people to be secured in their persons, their houses, their papers, and their other property, from all unreasonable searches and seizures, shall not be violated by warrants issued without probable cause, supported by oath or affirmation, or not particularly describing the places to be searched, or the persons or things to be seized.

With only minor changes, this sentence became the Fourth Amendment to the U.S. Constitution. It was ratified along with the other provisions of the Bill of Rights in 1791. The Fourth Amendment overcame the major objections to writs of assistance by stating that a warrant had to describe the place to be searched and the things to be seized. The warrant could not be issued arbitrarily, but only with "probable cause." In other words, there had to be reason to believe that the objects of the search or seizure were where the warrant said they were.

Still, the wording of the Fourth Amendment was vague. For instance, what exactly was a search? A seizure? What did "unreasonable'' mean? What was the role of the warrant? Could a search be reasonable without one? For 200 years, Americans—ordinary citizens, law-enforcement agents, lawyers, and judges—have been trying to answer questions like these. The chapters that follow describe some of the most important results of their efforts.

CHAPTER 2

Developing Some Principles

"The tendency of those who execute [carry out] the criminal laws of the country to obtain conviction by unlawful seizures . . . should find no sanction [approval] in the judgments of the courts."

JUSTICE WILLIAM R. DAY, in *Weeks* v. *United States* (1914)

They called him "Clubber" Williams. His real name was Alexander S. Williams, and he joined the New York City police force during the 1860s. Williams quickly rose to the rank of captain. He soon owned not only a house in the city but also a country estate in Connecticut, complete with a yacht. His tall, powerful body was a familiar sight around town. "I am so well known here in New York," he boasted, "that car horses [horses that pulled streetcars] nod to me mornings."

Why the nickname "Clubber"? Williams, like most of his fellow policemen at the time, made frequent use of his big billy club when dealing with the public. One journalist wrote vividly about the usual scene outside Williams's office at police headquarters:

Many a morning when I had nothing else to do I stood and saw the police bring in and kick out their bandaged, bloody prisoners, not

Nineteenth-century police officers with billy clubs. For most of the nineteenth century, the Supreme Court heard very few cases dealing with Fourth Amendment matters. For the most part, protection of citizens against unreasonable searches and seizures was left to the states and local governments. The Fourth Amendment was interpreted to mean protection only against actions taken by the federal government.

only strikers and foreigners, but thieves, too, and others of the miserable, friendless, troublesome poor.

The 1800s were a time when law enforcement in the United States was a rough business. Police officers might take almost anyone into custody, whether or not they had a reason to do so. Many police officers, especially in the West, had been in jail a few times themselves. The police could search people's living quarters freely. If someone objected, the billy club came in handy. One New York City superintendent admitted that his men often made arrests on suspicion and then hunted up evidence to make the arrests stick.

How could this be? Americans had bitterly attacked writs of assistance. After winning their independence from England, they had added the Bill of Rights to the Constitution in order to protect themselves against unreasonable searches and seizures. Why didn't this protection work against men like "Clubber" Williams?

The Role of the Supreme Court

As explained in the Foreword, the U.S. Supreme Court has the power of judicial review. This means that the Court can review laws passed by legislatures and decisions made by lower courts and then say whether or not they are constitutional. Laws and decisions may be weighed against any part of the Constitution. This, of course, includes the Bill of Rights, which protects citizens against abuses by the government.

The Supreme Court cannot simply decide that a government—such as the government of New York City, acting through "Clubber" Williams—is acting illegally. The Court can make a decision only when a specific case is brought before it. Here is how this procedure usually works: John or Jane Doe is prosecuted for a crime in a state or federal court. Doe loses the case, but believes that he or she was wrongly convicted. Doe thinks that the judge or jury misinterpreted (misunderstood) a federal law or the Constitution. So Doe asks the Supreme Court to review the case. If the justices agree to hear Doe's case, they will review it and reach a decision. They may affirm the lower court's decision, decide that the lower court was right. This means that Doe loses again. Or they may overturn the lower court's decision, conclude that the lower court was wrong. This means that the lower court's decision is reversed, and Doe wins. In that case, Doe either receives a new trial or goes free.

For the sake of simplicity, this book will speak of John Doe or Jane Doe (or whomever) as if he or she were acting alone. But, of course, Doe is represented by one or more lawyers. Often organizations play an important part, too. One organization that is especially active in cases involving the Bill of Rights is the American Civil Liberties Union (ACLU). Only the government has brought more cases before the Supreme Court than the ACLU has. Another organization that is very active in the field of civil rights is the National Association for the Advancement of Colored People (NAACP). Of all the organizations in the United States, the NAACP has the highest percentage of cases successfully argued before the Supreme Court.

For decades after the adoption of the Constitution, few of the cases decided by the Supreme Court involved the Bill of Rights and civil liberties. There were two main reasons for this: (1) According to the Supreme Court's own decisions, the Bill of Rights concerned only the *federal* government. As a result, the first ten amendments did not affect any *state* actions that might violate individual liberties. (2) The federal government was not involved in many criminal cases—cases involving crimes against society, such as robbery or murder, which are punished by the government. (In the other type of case, a civil case, private individuals or businesses sue each other over property or money.) Remember, since the Bill of Rights protects citizens against *government* abuse, most of its provisions concern criminal, not civil, cases.

Early Fourth Amendment Cases

John Burford didn't think he belonged in jail. He had been arrested by the authorities of Alexandria County. (During the early 1800s, the county was part of the District of Columbia. It is now in Virginia.) The arrest warrant was vague, however. It stated that Burford was

> *not of good name and fame*, nor of honest conversation, but an evil doer and disturber of the peace of the United States, so that murder, homicide, strifes, discords, and other grievances and damages, among the citizens of the United States, concerning their bodies and property, *are likely to arise thereby.*

Wasn't Burford's arrest unconstitutional? It amounted to seizure without "probable cause," because the warrant did not specify what Burford had done. The Supreme Court agreed. It gave reasons in its opinion (the written explanation that always accompanies a Supreme Court decision). Burford's arrest was a form of seizure, and this required "some good cause . . . supported by oath." Since the warrant failed this test, Burford was freed. This case—*ex parte Burford*—decided in 1806, was the first Supreme Court ruling on the Fourth Amendment. (*Ex parte* in the name of a court case means that the name following is that of the party that applied to have the case heard.)

Over the next eighty years, the Supreme Court dealt with just a handful of Fourth Amendment cases. One, in 1855, pointed out that the amendment did not apply to state laws. In another case of the same year, the Court made it clear that search and seizure involved only criminal, not civil, cases.

Two cases of the 1870s set up some additional guidelines. In one, the Supreme Court decided that the post office could not open letters and sealed packages without a warrant.

> The constitutional guaranty of the right of the people to be secure in their papers against unreasonable searches and seizures extends to their papers, thus closed against inspection, wherever they may be.

The next Fourth Amendment case had to do with "probable cause." Illegal whiskey had been seized from a man named Stacey.

The seizure itself was illegal, claimed Stacey, because the official acted out of malice, or ill will. This made no difference, said the Court:

> The question of malice or of good faith is not an element in the case. It is not a question of motive. If the facts and circumstances before the officer are such as to warrant a man of prudence [good judgment] and caution in believing that the offence has been committed, it is sufficient.

The decision went on to quote an earlier judge:

> Mr. Justice Washington says . . . "If malice is proved, yet if probable cause exists, there is no liability" [fault]. . . . He then defines probable cause in these words: "A reasonable ground of suspicion, supported by circumstances sufficiently strong in themselves to warrant a cautious man in the belief that the party is guilty of the offence with which he is charged."

The words that define "probable cause" have remained useful to this day.

Boyd, the First Important Decision

Thirty-five cases of plate glass . . . these gave rise to the first major Supreme Court decision involving the Fourth Amendment. The glass had been imported by New York merchants George and Edward Boyd, who had not paid the necessary taxes on it. When the Boyds were first tried in a federal district court, they were ordered to produce private financial records. Using these, the government was able to win its case.

The Boyds fought back, claiming that the district court had acted illegally in demanding their records. According to the Boyds, they had been the victims of an unreasonable search and seizure. Their case ended up in the Supreme Court as *Boyd* v. *United States*, decided in 1886. (The title shows that Boyd was the plaintiff, the party that brings the suit. The United States was the defendant, the party being sued. The *v.* stands for *versus*, the Latin word for "against.")

The Supreme Court agreed with the Boyds. In doing so, the justices made the Fourth Amendment a far more sweeping guarantee than it had been before. For one thing, the justices said that a search did not require actual entry into a person's house. The demand for records could be regarded as a search because it accomplished the same thing: It forced people to provide evidence against themselves.

The *Boyd* decision made another point as well. It said that the search was unreasonable because of its object, private financial records. The only things that officials could search and seize were goods that people should not possess. These included smuggled property, counterfeit money, or objects used to commit crimes, such as guns.

But a third point covered by the *Boyd* decision was the most important one of all. The Supreme Court said that forcing the Boyds to produce their private papers made them witnesses against themselves. This was forced self-incrimination, which is prohibited by the Fifth Amendment. Actually, the Court argued, the two amendments were closely related.

For the "unreasonable searches and seizures" condemned in the Fourth Amendment are almost always made for the purpose of compelling a man to give evidence against himself, which in criminal cases is condemned in the Fifth Amendment; and compelling a man "in a criminal case to be a witness against himself," which is condemned in the Fifth Amendment, throws light on the question as to what is an "unreasonable search and seizure" within the meaning of the Fourth Amendment.

To put it simply, the Supreme Court said that the search for the Boyds' financial records was illegal under the Fourth Amendment. It also said that allowing the records to be used as evidence was prohibited by the Fifth Amendment.

The decision in *Boyd* put teeth into the Fourth Amendment by providing a penalty if the amendment was violated. Law-enforcement officials would think twice about carrying out unreasonable searches and seizures if what they found could not be used as evidence in court.

The Privacy Issue

Mabel Warren liked to entertain. As the wife of a wealthy Boston lawyer, she enjoyed giving lavish parties. What she did *not* like, though, was the intense curiosity of her fellow Bostonians. The local newspapers found a big audience for detailed accounts of the Warrens' social life, illustrated with photographs. The photographers were certainly not invited to the Warrens' parties, but they could snap pictures from outside the grounds. They were aided by the camera technology of the day—the 1880s—which included such newfangled inventions as the telephoto lens.

Samuel Warren discussed these matters with his law partner, Louis D. Brandeis. The result was an important article the two men published in the *Harvard Law Review* in 1890, "The Right to Privacy."

> The press is overstepping in every direction the obvious bounds of propriety [good manners] and decency. Gossip is no longer the resource of the idle and of the vicious, but has become a trade, which is pursued with industry as well as effrontery [nerve]. . . . Man . . . has become more sensitive to publicity, so that solitude and privacy have become more essential to the individual; but modern enterprise and invention have, through invasions upon his privacy, subjected him to mental pain and distress, far greater than could be inflicted by mere bodily injury.

The two authors argued that the law should protect people's privacy, just as it protected their lives, liberty, and property, for "now the right to life has come to mean the right to enjoy life—the right to be let alone."

The American government, in its concern for the liberties of the individual, should work to guarantee this additional and essential right.

> The common law has always recognized a man's house as his castle. . . . Shall the courts thus close the front entrance to constituted authority [law enforcement], and open wide the back door to idle . . . curiosity?

In the years to come, this article was to be very important. The Constitution never mentions privacy. But the appeal by Brandeis and Warren made a big difference in interpreting the Fourth Amendment, and other portions of the Bill of Rights as well.

A Milestone of the Early 1900s

Could Americans gamble on lotteries in the early 1900s? Not legally. A lot of people liked the idea of buying chances in the hope of winning a jackpot. But this kind of gambling was often linked to organized crime. The states had laws against lotteries. A federal law had even made it illegal to send lottery tickets through the mail.

Fremont Weeks had been sent to jail for doing just that. At his trial, the prosecution introduced evidence, including lottery tickets, that played a big part in convicting him. Weeks, however, said that this evidence had been obtained illegally. The police had no warrant. They broke into his house while he was at work. They took not only the lottery tickets but also stock certificates, insurance policies, and all sorts of private letters and papers. Weeks claimed that this was an illegal search and seizure, making it contrary to the Fourth Amendment. He asked for the return of his papers before the trial began, but his request was turned down.

The Supreme Court agreed to review the *Weeks* case. In 1914, it handed down a decision in Weeks's favor. The opinion stated in part:

> If letters and private documents can thus be seized and held and used in evidence against a citizen accused of an offense, the

protection of the 4th Amendment, declaring his right to be secure against such searches and seizures, is of no value, and, so far as those thus placed are concerned, might as well be stricken [removed] from the Constitution.

The Court's opinion went on to say:

We therefore reach the conclusion that the letters in question were taken from the house of the accused by an official of the United States, acting under color [authority] of his office, in direct violation of the constitutional rights of the defendant. . . . In holding [the papers] and permitting their use upon the trial, we think prejudicial error was committed.

In other words, the prosecution in the lower court had spoiled its case—committed "prejudicial error"—by using illegally seized evidence at the trial.

In the case of *Weeks* v. *United States*, the Supreme Court strengthened the idea that was first suggested in the *Boyd* decision. This was the notion that illegally seized evidence has no place in a federal criminal trial. The Court's decision also made it clear that the Fourth Amendment did not have to be linked to the Fifth Amendment in order to be effective. Since the time of *Weeks*, the principle of rejecting evidence that was seized illegally has come to be known as the exclusionary rule. ("Exclusionary" comes from the word *exclude*, which means "keep out.")

The exclusionary rule, one expert has written,

infused [injected] life into the hitherto [until now] lifeless body of the Fourth Amendment. This process, begun . . . in the Boyd case, had achieved fruition [developed fully] in the Weeks case. There remained questions to be answered, but the most important answer had been given: [T]he Fourth Amendment would not become a forgotten provision of the Bill of Rights.

The exclusionary rule has been both praised and criticized since it was adopted. It will be treated separately in Chapter 8.

CHAPTER 3

Law in a Lawless Era

"The damnable character of the 'bootlegger's' business should not
close our eyes to the mischief which will surely follow any attempt to
destroy it by unwarranted [improper] methods."

JUSTICE JAMES C. McREYNOLDS,
in *Carroll* v. *United States* (1928)

Wayne Bidwell Wheeler was born on a farm in Ohio. Like most
people, he was strongly influenced by certain events of his child-
hood. What most affected Wheeler in his early years—the 1870s
and 1880s—was drinking. His uncle, who lived a mile away, spent
many nights in the village saloon. He would return home in his
wagon and often fall off, drunk out of his senses. When the horses
turned up with an empty wagon, the entire family, helped by
neighbors, had to search the countryside for the missing man.

This was bad enough. But even worse was an accident involving
Wheeler himself. One day the young boy was working in the fields
with a group of farmers cutting hay. As the harvesters mowed, they
gathered bundles of hay with their pitchforks and heaved them up
onto a wagon. Working near Wheeler was a farmhand who had had
too much to drink. Suddenly the man's pitchfork slipped, and one
of the tines plunged right into the young boy's leg. With blood

---

"The Drunkard's Progress." This nineteenth-century illustration shows the
fate that awaited those who drank too much. The ratification of the Eighteenth Amendment in 1919 resulted in national Prohibition in 1920. The
federal government's attempt to stop the sale and transport of liquor led to
many legal disputes about what were unreasonable searches and seizures.

streaming from his wound, Wheeler exclaimed: "I hope that some day there won't be any more liquor to make men drunk!"

Before many years passed, Wheeler began to do everything he could to make this day a reality. As soon as he was graduated from college, he went to work for the Anti-Saloon League. The organization had been founded just a few months earlier, in 1893. Its aim was prohibition—outlawing the manufacture and sale of alcoholic beverages.

The "Dry" Years

Americans had always been heavy drinkers. During colonial times, alcoholic beverages were a part of almost every social occasion, from christenings to burials. Gradually, however, many Americans began to realize that drinking to excess was harmful to health, safety, and family life. Some people believed that the only way to cut down on heavy drinking was to outlaw alcohol altogether. They organized the temperance movement, whose goal was prohibition. One of the most important groups was the Women's Christian Temperance Union (WCTU). Another temperance group was the Anti-Saloon League.

Spurred by temperance groups, many towns, counties, and states went "dry," or adopted prohibition. By the time of World War I, the temperance movement had won enough support to establish national Prohibition. This was done through a new constitutional amendment. The Eighteenth Amendment was ratified in 1919. It prohibited the making, transporting, and selling of alcoholic beverages. When this amendment went into effect in 1920, Wheeler's Anti-Saloon League proclaimed the birth of a new nation, "an era of clear thinking and clean living!"

This was not to be, however. On the whole, Prohibition was a failure. The amount of alcohol people drank did decrease. The number of people suffering from alcoholism apparently declined, too. But millions of Americans went right on drinking because they didn't see anything wrong with it. A huge illegal business sprang up. Bootleggers, the people who ran it, made alcoholic beverages and also smuggled them into the United States from abroad. Americans who wanted liquor either bought it from bootleggers or at illegal saloons known as speakeasies.

Crime organizations, or syndicates, made millions of dollars smuggling and selling illegal liquor. Gang warfare broke out in most major cities as rival syndicates fought to control local bootlegging. The number of murders, for instance, doubled between 1920 and 1930. Probably the worst aspect of national Prohibition was that it turned millions of ordinary Americans into criminals. Whenever they bought alcoholic drinks, they broke the law. They lost respect not only for the laws that enforced Prohibition but for the idea of law itself.

The Case of the Stopped Car

During the era of national Prohibition, Fourth Amendment cases multiplied. Why? Because people accused of dealing in illegal alcohol were breaking *federal* law. This led to an increase in searches and seizures by federal law-enforcement agencies, such as the Federal Bureau of Investigation (FBI). As a result, more search and seizure cases ended up before the Supreme Court. New decisions shed new light on the application of the Fourth Amendment. Keep in mind, however, that at this time the Fourth Amendment applied only to federal cases. State governments were not bound to protect Fourth Amendment rights unless required to do so by their own constitutions or laws.

The case of George Carroll was special because he was driving a car. Today we take automobiles for granted, but they were not so common during the 1920s. Only a few years earlier, cars cost so much that only the rich could afford them. Then Henry Ford began manufacturing inexpensive automobiles. By 1921, when this story begins, cars were just beginning to clog the nation's roads. There were no good highways, almost no service stations, and few legal restrictions on driving or drivers.

Carroll was driving near Grand Rapids, Michigan, when he was stopped by federal Prohibition agents. They searched Carroll's car, found liquor hidden under the seat, and arrested him. After he was convicted, Carroll appealed the decision. He argued that the search of his car was unreasonable because the officers did not have a warrant. The Supreme Court disagreed. Yes, a search without a warrant was usually regarded as unreasonable. But an exception should be made for moving vehicles. In this situation, getting a search warrant wasn't practical. A warrant had to specify a particular place, and a car could of course quickly be driven away from any given area.

This did not mean, the justices said, that *any* car could be stopped. Automobiles, like houses and other buildings, are protected against unreasonable searches and seizures. A search without a warrant can take place only if there is probable cause for it. Probable cause did exist in this case, said the Supreme Court, because Carroll was known to be a bootlegger. In addition, he was driving in a state that had borders with Canada. A great deal of liquor was smuggled across those borders.

Carroll v. *United States*, decided by the Supreme Court in 1925, set an important precedent. (A precedent is a ruling that guides future court decisions.) Since then, it has generally been legal, given probable cause, to stop moving automobiles and search them without a warrant.

The Case of the Speakeasy Search

From the point of view of the Fourth Amendment, the battle against bootlegging involved several different issues. One, just described, had to do with moving vehicles. The Supreme Court's *Carroll* decision opened the way for warrantless searches of cars in motion. Another issue concerned arrests. It has long been common practice for police officers to search the person they are arresting, mainly to protect themselves against concealed weapons. But what

New York State troopers stop suspected bootleggers in 1921. The Supreme Court ruled in 1925 that automobiles could be halted and searched without a warrant under certain circumstances. That might be the case if police wanted to preserve evidence of a crime and thought that the car was going to be driven out of an area where the police and courts had power—across a border, for example.

about nearby premises? Is a warrant necessary in order to search them?

A raid on a California speakeasy provided a partial answer to this question. Prohibition agents swooped down on the saloon one October day in 1924. They had an arrest warrant that allowed them to take the bartender, a man named Birdsall, into custody. They also had a search warrant to look for "intoxicating liquors and articles for their manufacture." While searching for these, the agents found a ledger. This account book listed supplies, receipts, and expenses (including gifts to police officers). The ledger indicated that Joseph Marron was the actual owner of the speakeasy. On the basis of this evidence, Marron was tried and found guilty.

He appealed the decision. He argued that since the search warrant did not mention the ledger, the agents had no right to seize it.

The Supreme Court rejected Marron's appeal in 1927. The justices agreed that the search warrant did not authorize seizing the ledger. But, they said, the *arrest* warrant did. Birdsall was carrying on a "criminal enterprise"—running a speakeasy. Arresting him was therefore lawful. So was searching the premises in order to find and seize the things that were used to carry on the illegal activity. According to the Court's opinion in *Marron* v. *United States* (1927), the ledger may not have been on Birdsall's person at the time of his arrest. But, the Court noted:

> [The ledger] was in his immediate possession and control. The authority of officers to search and seize the things by which the nuisance [the criminal activity] was being maintained extended to all parts of the premises used for the unlawful purpose.

Here the Court was indicating that law-enforcement agents could carry out far-reaching searches incidental to—in connection with—a valid arrest. This type of situation therefore became another exception to the principle that a reasonable search requires a search warrant.

The Case of the "Whispering Wires"

"Hello. Say, this is George Christy of the dry squad. Is the Commander there?"

"No, Roy isn't here."

"Well, have you got the place at 2014 Third Avenue cleaned up? We'll have to go up there."

"All right, Christy. Comstock called up awhile ago and told me about it and I told him to go up there."

What's going on is this: George Christy, a Prohibition enforcement agent, is calling Roy Olmstead on the telephone. Olmstead is known as "the Commander" because he controls a bootlegging organization. Christy speaks to an associate of Olmstead's. He warns him that there's going to be a raid on a speakeasy ("the place at 2014 Third Avenue"). Thus alerted, Olmstead's people—men like Comstock—can hide the evidence before the raid takes place.

Olmstead operated a big illegal liquor business out of Seattle, Washington. He knew the ways of law-enforcement agents, since he had been one himself. (And, clearly, he had other agents on his payroll.) What he did not know was that his phone had been tapped by the authorities. Using wiretapped conversations as evidence, the federal government arrested and tried Olmstead.

People called Olmstead's case the "Whispering Wires Case." Like automobiles, telephones had only recently become common. The public now realized that voices could not only travel great distances, but they could also be overheard without the speakers' knowledge. Americans were fascinated by the new technology of wiretapping. (This is a way of eavesdropping on phone conversations by attaching a wire or additional electrical connection to a telephone line.) The court found the evidence compelling, too. Olmstead was convicted and sent to jail.

Olmstead's lawyers appealed his case to the Supreme Court. They argued that wiretapping was illegal. The officials, they said, had no warrant and had therefore conducted a form of unreasonable search and seizure. In the case of *Olmstead* v. *United States*, decided in 1928, the Court held otherwise.

Chief Justice William Howard Taft (a former U.S. president) wrote:

The [Fourth] Amendment itself shows that the search is to be of material things—the person, the house, his papers or his effects [movable property]. The description of the warrant necessary to make the proceeding lawful is that it must specify the place to be searched and the person or *things* to be seized. . . . The Amendment does not forbid what was done here. There was no searching. There was no seizure. The evidence was secured by the use of the sense of hearing and that only. There was no entry of the houses or offices of the defendants.

Taft went on to say that it would not make sense to extend Fourth Amendment protections to include "telephone wires reaching to the whole world." And he added that the Fourth Amendment cannot be

> violated as against a defendant unless there has been an official search and seizure of his person or such a seizure of his papers or his tangible material effects or an actual physical invasion of his house . . . for the purpose of making a seizure.

By ruling that wiretap evidence was legal, the Supreme Court upheld (supported) Olmstead's conviction. But the decision of the Court was not unanimous. This means that all nine justices did not agree with it. Court decisions are reached by a majority vote. The opinion that expresses the majority's reasoning is referred to as the Court opinion. But as many as four justices may dissent, or disagree. This is what happened in the *Olmstead* case. It was the first search case to be decided by such a close vote (5 to 4).

One of the dissenting voices on the Court was that of Justice Louis D. Brandeis. He wrote an opinion explaining his position. (Any justice, whether in the majority or the minority, can write an opinion on a case.) Brandeis's opinion included this passage:

> The progress of science in furnishing the government with means of espionage [spying] is not likely to stop with wire-tapping. Ways may some day be developed by which the government, without removing papers from secret drawers, can reproduce them in court, and by which it will be enabled to expose to a jury the most intimate occurrences of the home. Can it be that the Constitution affords no protection against such invasions of individual security?

Brandeis went on to warn against government spying even when it is done for a good cause:

> It is . . . immaterial [unimportant] that the intrusion was in aid of law enforcement. Experience should teach us to be most on our guard to

Associate Justice Louis D. Brandeis served on the Supreme Court from 1916 to 1939. In his dissenting opinion in *Olmstead* v. *United States* (1928), Brandeis wrote that "decency, security, and liberty alike demand that government officials [should] be subjected to the same rules of conduct that are commands to the citizen."

protect liberty when the government's purposes are beneficent [well-meaning]. Men born to freedom are naturally alert to repel invasion of their liberty by evil-minded rulers. The greatest dangers to liberty lurk in insidious encroachment [sneaky advances] by men of zeal, well-meaning, but without understanding.

As it turned out, the *Olmstead* case did not settle the legal issue of wiretapping for long. The story of electronic surveillance in the years since 1928 is told in Chapter 7.

Changing Times

"There is no war between the Constitution and common sense."
JUSTICE TOM CLARK, in *Mapp* v. *Ohio* (1961)

President Herbert Hoover called national Prohibition a "noble experiment." By the 1930s, however, Americans were tired of experimenting. Congress and the states repealed Prohibition with the Twenty-first Amendment, ratified in 1933.

By this time, the United States was in the midst of a terrible economic slump, the Great Depression. Millions of people lost their jobs. Many banks failed, and people lost their life savings. Homeless families camped out in cardboard shacks. Hungry men and women waited for hours in breadlines just to get a piece of bread and a bowl of soup.

To cope with hard times, the government became much more involved in its citizens' everyday lives than it had ever been before. It set up relief programs to provide jobs, housing, and food. It started the Social Security system to help the elderly and the disabled.

American society was going through big changes. So were its laws and its courts. To understand how these changes affected the

Chief Justice Earl Warren served on the Supreme Court from 1953 to 1969. He led the Court in a number of important decisions that extended the rights of citizens, including the rights of those accused in criminal cases.

Bill of Rights, especially the Fourth Amendment, it is necessary to step back in time.

Extending Citizen Protections

Twenty-three cases of severe and inhuman beating and whipping of men; four of beating and shooting; two of robbing and shooting; three of robbing; five men shot and killed; two shot and wounded; four beaten to death; one beaten and roasted.

This appalling catalog of crimes was a partial list of attacks on newly freed African Americans. It was compiled by a government agent in one small district of Kentucky in 1865, right after the Civil War. The war had ended slavery. But many former slaves now found themselves at the mercy of certain violent white southerners. They seemed determined to do anything to keep blacks "in their place"—inferior to whites.

To protect the newly freed African Americans, the Fourteenth Amendment was added to the Constitution in 1868. It indicated that the former slaves were citizens, then stated:

No State shall make or enforce any law which shall abridge [reduce or take away] the privileges or immunities [safeguards] of citizens of the United States; nor shall any State deprive any person of life, liberty, or property, without due process of law.

The wording in the second half of this sentence is almost exactly the same as that of a similar passage in the Fifth Amendment. But there's an important difference. Here, it is the *states* that are warned against violating a person's right to life, liberty, and property.

Until this time, the Supreme Court had held that the Bill of Rights did not apply to state governments. Now it seemed logical that the Fourteenth Amendment would extend the guarantees of the Bill of Rights to the state level. After all, people as citizens of the

United States had these rights, and the states were now forbidden to deprive citizens of their rights. The Supreme Court didn't see it that way, however. For decades, the Fourteenth Amendment's due process clause served mainly to protect businesses against government interference. Court decisions held that corporations were to be regarded as "persons." Unwanted regulations were seen as depriving these "persons" of their property rights.

It was not until the twentieth century that this situation began to change. The first breakthrough came in the 1925 case of *Gitlow* v. *New York*. This case involved the free speech provision of the First Amendment. In its decision, the Supreme Court stated that the due process clause protected "fundamental personal rights" against state infringement, or interference. This decision began the process of incorporation—that is, incorporating (including) the Bill of Rights into the phrase "due process of law."

Over the next twelve years, incorporation was extended to several other Bill of Rights guarantees: freedom of the press (1931), the right to counsel (a lawyer) in a criminal trial involving murder or other serious offenses (1932), freedom of religion (1934 and 1940), and freedom of assembly (1937).

Fourth Amendment Confusion

What happened to the protection the Bill of Rights guarantees against unreasonable searches and seizures? In decisions of this period, the Supreme Court made it clear that it did not regard all the protections of the Bill of Rights as equal. Some rights, such as those protected by the First Amendment, were viewed as "fundamental principles of liberty and justice which lie at the base of all our civil and political institutions." Others, such as those protected by the Fourth and Fifth Amendments, were regarded as "not of the essence of [not basic to] a scheme of ordered liberty."

This distinction led to some confusion. A case in point was that of Julius Wolf. This Denver doctor was suspected of performing abortions. (At the time of the events described—the 1940s—

abortion was illegal in the United States.) A deputy sheriff raided Wolf's office without a warrant. There he found appointment records that were incriminating—that is, the records indicated that crimes had occurred. After patients were questioned, Wolf was tried and found guilty. He appealed on the grounds that the search was illegal and that the materials should not have been used against him.

The Supreme Court both agreed and disagreed with Wolf's argument. Justice Felix Frankfurter wrote the Court's opinion in *Wolf* v. *Colorado*, a decision handed down in 1949. First he stated, "The security of one's privacy against arbitrary intrusion by the police—which is at the core of the Fourth Amendment—is basic to a free society." Because of the due process clause, the states were obliged to protect this basic right. Frankfurter condemned "the knock at the door, whether by day or by night, as a prelude to a search, without authority of law but solely on the authority of the police." If a state approved of such conduct, said Frankfurter, it would certainly violate the Fourteenth Amendment.

The Supreme Court therefore agreed that the search of Wolf's office had been illegal. But it disagreed about admitting the seized evidence in court. At that time, illegally seized evidence was kept out of federal criminal trials. But Frankfurter refused to apply the exclusionary rule to the states. He noted that "most of the English-speaking world" did not regard this protection as necessary. Indeed, common law had long held that evidence pointing to guilt in criminal cases could be introduced in court no matter how it had been obtained. Certainly many judges opposed the exclusionary rule. One of them was Benjamin Cardozo. As a judge in New York State (before he joined the Supreme Court in 1932), Cardozo had ruled against applying the rule at the state level. In doing so, he asked—in a phrase that became famous—whether "the criminal is to go free because the constable [police officer] had blundered?"

At the time of the *Wolf* decision, some states had adopted the exclusionary rule, but most had not. Colorado was one of the states that had not done so. Frankfurter wrote:

Granting that in practice the exclusion of evidence may be an effective way of deterring [discouraging] unreasonable searches, it is not for this Court to condemn . . . a State's reliance upon other methods which, if consistently enforced, would be equally effective.

What were these "other methods"? For one thing, people who believed that they had been the victims of unreasonable searches or seizures could sue the police. The main point, Frankfurter said, was that public opinion worked better at the local and state levels than at the federal level. This kind of pressure should be effective in restraining police officers who overstepped the bounds of fairness.

The *Wolf* decision left the meaning of the Fourth Amendment uncertain. Its basic principle—the guarantee against unlawful searches and seizures—applied to the states. But the basic means of enforcement—the exclusionary rule—did not.

A Landmark of the 1960s

"I would like the Court to be remembered as the people's court," said Chief Justice Earl Warren when he retired. He had served as chief justice of the United States from 1953 to 1969, a period in Supreme Court history known as the Warren Court.

Many observers agree that the American people have benefited greatly from the landmark decisions handed down by the Warren Court. (A landmark decision is one of great importance.) Others, however, believe that the Court went too far. The Supreme Court, say these critics, should show judicial restraint—confine itself to settling disputes. The Warren Court, such critics argue, began a modern trend toward judicial activism—actually making policy. The disagreement between these two points of view is an old one, and it continues today.

There is little doubt about one thing, however: An early case decided by the Warren Court, *Brown* v. *Board of Education of Topeka* (1954), was one of the most important cases in American

Associate Justice Felix Frankfurter served on the Supreme Court from 1939 to 1962. In his majority opinion in *Wolf* v. *Colorado* (1949), Frankfurter ruled that the Fourth Amendment protected citizens against unreasonable searches and seizures by the states. However, Frankfurter argued that the Constitution did not protect citizens from the *use* of illegally seized evidence in state trials.

history. The Supreme Court's decision outlawed the racial segregation that was then legal in the nation's public schools. Two years later, the Court ruled that segregated buses were illegal. (This case grew out of the Montgomery, Alabama, bus boycott led by Martin Luther King, Jr.)

Other landmark decisions of the Warren Court dealt with the separation of church and state, and with political equality. In 1962, the Supreme Court ruled against state-sponsored prayers in public schools. Another 1962 decision required that voters should be represented equally in legislative districts.

Still another major area of Warren Court activism was the trend toward incorporation—extending the protections guaranteed in the Bill of Rights to the states—begun in the 1930s. In 1961, it was the turn of the Fourth Amendment to be incorporated. This is how it happened: One May morning in 1957, the police showed up at the Cleveland home of a woman named Dollree Mapp. According to a tip the officers had gotten, she was hiding a man wanted for questioning in a recent bombing. Also, she was suspected of running an illegal gambling operation. The police had no warrant. Mapp refused to let them in. Several hours later they returned, broke into the house, and showed Mapp what they said was a warrant. (Their claim was apparently not valid, because no warrant was produced at the trial.)

Over Mapp's objections, the officers ransacked her house. They did not find the man they were looking for. Nor did they find any evidence of gambling. In a basement trunk, however, they did find some "lewd and lascivious books and pictures"—that is, pornography. When the books and pictures were introduced in court, Mapp was convicted under an Ohio law that prohibited the possession of obscene materials. Mapp appealed to the Supreme Court. She claimed that the search was unreasonable; so the materials seized were inadmissable (could not be used at the trial). In a 5 to 4 decision, the Court agreed. According to the majority opinion in *Mapp* v. *Ohio* (1961):

> Since the Fourth Amendment's right of privacy has been declared enforceable against the States through the Due Process Clause of the Fourteenth, it is enforceable against them by the same sanction of exclusion as is used against the Federal Government.

In other words, the case of *Wolf* v. *Colorado* (1949) had incorporated the Fourth Amendment's guarantee against unreasonable searches and seizures into the Fourteenth Amendment. Now this incorporation would be enforced by the exclusionary rule.

> Our holding that the exclusionary rule is an essential part of both the Fourth and Fourteenth Amendments is not only the logical dictate [rule] of prior cases, but it also makes very good sense. There is no war between the Constitution and common sense. Presently, a

A detective escorts Dollree Mapp into police headquarters in New York City in 1970. Illegal drugs had been found in her apartment. Nine years earlier, in the landmark Supreme Court decision in *Mapp* v. *Ohio,* the justices (voting 6 to 3) had ruled that evidence obtained by illegal searches and seizures could not be used in state trials.

federal prosecutor may make no use of evidence illegally seized, but a State's attorney across the street may, although he supposedly is operating under the same Amendment. Thus the State, by admitting evidence unlawfully seized, serves to encourage disobedience to the Federal Constitution which it is bound to uphold. . . . Having once recognized that the right to privacy embodied in [made part of] the Fourth Amendment is enforceable against the States, and that the right to be secure against rude invasions of privacy by state officers is, therefore, constitutional in origin, we can no longer permit that right to remain an empty promise.

In 1949, the justices had rejected applying the exclusionary rule to the states. Why had the Supreme Court changed its position in 1961? One reason, according to the Court, was that the majority of the states now had some form of exclusionary rule. Second, other remedies against unreasonable searches and seizures—such as local public opinion—appeared to be, in the Court's words, "worthless and futile."

Rights of the Accused—and a Backlash

With *Mapp*, it was as if a door had been flung open. Before 1961, incorporation decisions had dealt mainly with First Amendment rights, such as freedom of speech, freedom of the press, and freedom of religion. After the *Mapp* case, attention became focused on the rights of the accused as guaranteed by the Fifth, Sixth, and Eighth Amendments. State trials now had to guarantee rights that had previously been protected only at the federal level. In *Gideon* v. *Wainwright* (1963), the Supreme Court held that anyone on trial for a serious crime has the right to have a lawyer. The decision in *Malloy* v. *Hogan* (1964) protects an accused person from forced self-incrimination. In *Klopfer* v. *North Carolina* (1967), the Court ruled that the accused has the right to a speedy trial.

These Warren Court decisions of the 1960s had a tremendous impact. Most criminal cases—well over 90 percent—are handled by the states. For this reason, what has been called the due process revolution had a direct effect on most trials for murder and other violent crimes. In the words of one observer:

Prior to 1961 each state had virtually [almost entirely] gone its own way on criminal procedure, administering criminal justice with the degree of . . . muscle that suited the style of its people, and with little regard for the Constitution and courts of the United States. The Warren Court had undertaken to bridle [control] that process, to make it more humane and evenhanded.

Ironically, however, this "revolution" happened at a time when crime was increasing. Take the four violent crimes of murder, rape, robbery, and aggravated assault. People were shocked by statistics on the crime rate—the number of these crimes per 100,000 Americans. FBI information indicated that, for these four offenses, the rate more than doubled between 1957 and 1967. The 1960s were also a period of urban riots, uprisings on college campuses, and protests against the Vietnam War.

By the late 1960s, a backlash had developed. Many Americans accused the courts, especially the Supreme Court, of "coddling" criminals. These critics believed that decisions that strengthened the rights of the accused were helping wrongdoers at the expense of law-abiding citizens. The exlusionary rule came under special attack. (These criticisms are discussed in Chapter 8.)

When Richard Nixon ran for president against Hubert Humphrey and George Wallace in 1968, his campaign theme was the need for a return to "law and order." He denounced the Supreme Court's decisions in such cases as *Mapp*. Nixon said: "Some of our courts and their decisions . . . have gone too far in weakening the peace forces as against the criminal forces in this country." Whatever the truth of his attacks, Nixon's message appealed to voters. He won the election.

Nixon took several steps to strengthen law enforcement. One was the Omnibus Crime Control and Safe Streets Act of 1968. Among other things, this law passed by Congress gave the government broad wiretapping powers. (The law is discussed in greater detail in Chapter 7.) Another bill, passed in 1970, was aimed at controlling crime in Washington, D.C. Its most controversial provision allowed the police to obtain search warrants that enabled them to enter any premises without announcing themselves. This "no-knock" law aroused a great deal of opposition. As it happened, very few "no-knock" warrants were issued, and the provision was soon repealed.

Nixon also had a chance to make changes in the Supreme Court. When Chief Justice Warren resigned, the president appointed a new chief justice, Warren E. Burger. Critics of the Warren Court hoped that the Supreme Court would now be more sympathetic to law enforcement. But it has been difficult to tell whether there has been a steady trend in one direction. This is certainly true of the Fourth Amendment. The next four chapters will examine specific areas of Fourth Amendment interpretation from the late 1960s to the present.

Search and Seizure: Personal Privacy

"The message is, Be careful of what you put in the garbage."
LAW PROFESSOR GRAHAM HUGHES

On the night of April 23, 1973, Herbert Giglotto and his wife were asleep in their apartment in Collinsville, Illinois. Suddenly they were awakened by a gang of men who had broken down two doors to get in. The men handcuffed the Giglottos, pointed guns at them, and ransacked the apartment. That same night, there were similar break-ins at the homes of five other families in the Collinsville area.

A crime spree? Hardly. The raiders were federal narcotics agents. They had no search warrants and no arrest warrants. What's more, they had broken into the wrong homes. They found no drugs and made no arrests. Several months later, the agents were tried and acquitted. The charge against them—conspiracy to deprive citizens of their constitutional rights—was a vague one that the prosecution was unable to prove.

This law-enforcement officer uses a dog to help find illegal drugs. In 1983, the Supreme Court ruled that the use of dogs to perform canine "sniff tests" to find drugs was properly limited and so could not be considered a Fourth Amendment search. If a police officer is in a place where he or she has a right to be, no search warrant is needed for dogs to assist in the search for evidence such as drugs.

The Collinsville episode shocked the public and outraged the Giglottos and their fellow townspeople. It also provoked explanations from law-enforcement agents. One of these agents said:

> You see these vermin selling drugs and what they do to people and our cities and you get sickened and angry and perhaps you take your hostilities and frustrations out on some guy's bookcase. It's not right. But how are you going to prevent it?

The real culprit in cases like this—and there were others—wasn't the drug-enforcement program or its agents. It was drugs and their hold on American society.

"Public Enemy No. 1"

"Public Enemy No. 1" is what President Richard M. Nixon called drug abuse. Many Americans agreed with him. Within just a few short years, drugs had become a grave national concern.

The drug problem mainly concerned illegal drugs, such as marijuana and heroin. These drugs had not been widely used before the mid-1960s. At that time, however, marijuana became popular among teenagers and young adults. During the 1970s and 1980s, the more expensive cocaine became a status symbol for rich professionals, sports stars, and entertainers. During the mid-1980s, a new and cheaper form of smokable cocaine, crack, swept through many inner-city neighborhoods. By the late 1980s, it was estimated that 23 million Americans were regular users of illegal drugs. The United States had the highest rate of drug abuse of any industrialized nation.

Experts disagreed on why drug use had increased. They also disagreed about the health hazards of the various illegal substances. But they did agree on at least three points: (1) Drug abuse endangers work performance and destroys personal relationships. (2) The use of shared needles to inject drugs spreads such diseases as hepatitis B and AIDS (acquired immune deficiency syndrome).

(3) Drugs and crime are closely related. The main reason for this is that possession of drugs is defined as a crime. Also, drug users may turn to crime in order to get the money they need to support their habit. Finally, because of the enormous profits to be made from making and selling illegal drugs, drug dealers shoot and kill in their efforts to control and extend their markets. (The drug epidemic was accompanied by a big increase in the number of illegal handguns.)

The government has tried several different approaches in its attempt to win what it calls the "war on drugs." It works mainly through the Drug Enforcement Administration (DEA). Because much of the illegal supply comes from outside the country, DEA agents try to intercept and destroy drugs that are being smuggled in. They also try to destroy drug laboratories and supplies, to smash drug networks, and to imprison the "drug lords" who direct the operations. All of these law-enforcement activities have a direct bearing on the search-and-seizure provisions of the Fourth Amendment. For this reason, many of the cases discussed in this chapter and the three that follow involve drugs, drug traffic, and illegal weapons.

This chapter focuses on the Fourth Amendment as it relates to personal privacy, with drugs as a major, but not the only, concern. As always, the courts must take a balancing approach. They walk a fine line between guaranteeing individual rights and protecting the community. The case of the Giglottos and their neighbors never reached the Supreme Court. But other cases that have been reviewed by the Court since then deal with a wide range of privacy issues, from street searches to invasions of the human body itself.

Stop and Frisk

Almost anyone who has watched a few movie or television crime dramas has seen the practice known as "stop and frisk." Typically, police officer John Brown stops citizen Bob Green and pats him down (runs his hands lightly over Green's body). Brown is usually looking for concealed weapons. What are Green's rights?

It is interesting that the Supreme Court handed down two decisions having to do with this very question on the same day in 1968. One, *Terry* v. *Ohio*, hinged on the actions of Cleveland policeman Martin McFadden. After observing John Terry and a friend for several minutes, McFadden was convinced that they were "casing" a store and planning a robbery. He stopped Terry, frisked him, and found a revolver. Terry was tried and convicted of carrying a concealed weapon. He appealed to a higher Ohio court. His appeal was dismissed on the grounds that there was no "substantial constitutional question." Stop and frisk, said the Ohio court, was not the same as search and seizure (or, to be exact, seizure and search).

The U.S. Supreme Court ruled otherwise, however.

There is some suggestion in the use of such terms as "stop" and "frisk" that such police conduct is outside the purview [scope] of the Fourth Amendment because neither action arises to the level of a "search" or "seizure" within the meaning of the Constitution. We emphatically reject this notion. It is quite plain that the Fourth Amendment governs "seizures" of the person which do not eventuate [end up] in a trip to the station house and prosecution for crime—"arrests" in traditional terminology [the words commonly used]. It must be recognized that whenever a police officer accosts [stops] an individual and restrains his freedom to walk away, he has "seized" that person. And it is nothing less than sheer torture of the English language to suggest that a careful exploration of the outer surfaces of a person's clothing all over his or her body in an attempt to find weapons is not a "search."

If this stop and frisk did indeed amount to search and seizure, did it violate the Fourth Amendment? Terry argued that it did, because McFadden didn't have *probable* cause. The Court, however, decided that probable cause was not necessary. The officer's conduct was *reasonable* under the circumstances, and that was what mattered.

Each case of this sort will, of course, have to be decided on its own facts. We merely hold today that where a police officer observes unusual conduct which leads him reasonably to conclude in light of his experience that criminal activity may be afoot and that the persons with whom he is dealing may be armed and presently dangerous . . . he is entitled for the protection of himself and others in the area to conduct a carefully limited search of the outer clothing of such persons in an attempt to discover weapons which might be used to assault him.

Such a search is a reasonable search under the Fourth Amendment, and any weapons seized may properly be introduced in evidence against the person from whom they were taken.

The *Terry* decision created important precedents. It settled the question of whether stop and frisk was covered by Fourth Amendment guarantees. It also set a standard of reasonableness, rather than probable cause, for certain kinds of search and seizure. Reasonable suspicion is a more flexible standard than probable cause.

The other stop-and-frisk decision handed down on the same day as *Terry* involved drugs. A New York City policeman, Anthony Martin, spotted a heroin addict named Nelson Sibron in a restaurant. After watching Sibron talking to other addicts, Martin called him outside. "You know what I'm after," said the officer. Sibron reached into his pocket, and so did Martin. Out came several envelopes containing heroin.

The situation here was quite different from the one in the *Terry* case. In *Sibron* v. *New York* (1968), the Court ruled

[t]he search was not reasonably limited in scope to the accomplishment of the only goal which might conceivably have justified its inception [beginning]—the protection of the officer by disarming a potentially dangerous man. Such a search violates the guarantee of the Fourth Amendment.

Police stop and frisk several suspects during a raid on suspected illegal drug dealers. A frisk consisting of a "pat-down" of the outside of someone's clothing is considered a "search," according to a 1968 Supreme Court ruling. But if reasonable circumstances, such as the need to act quickly, require it, such a procedure may be carried out without a warrant.

The search of Sibron was unconstitutional because it did not involve the officer's concern for his own safety. For this reason, Sibron's conviction was overturned.

These two decisions—*Terry* and *Sibron*—have governed most later stop-and-frisk situations. Many of these involve automobiles; such cases are discussed further in Chapter 6.

Homes and Other Premises

One reason the Giglottos' nightmare aroused such a storm of protest was that they were at home—safe, they thought, from intrusion. The Supreme Court tends to be especially protective of Fourth Amendment rights when citizens are in their homes or on other private premises. A warrant is usually required if the circumstances allow it.

Traditionally, however, there has been more leeway when searches are incidental to a valid arrest. Even here, though, the Court has been cautious in recent years. The case of *Chimel* v. *California* (1969) put limits on the searches allowed under the 1927 *Marron* decision (see Chapter 3). In the *Chimel* case, officers without a warrant had entered the home of a suspected burglar and legally arrested him. They went on to ransack not only his entire house but also his attic, garage, and workshop. This would not do, the Supreme Court said. Such a search could not extend beyond the arrested person's "immediate control" or "grabbing distance"— that is, the area in which he or she could reach a weapon or destroy evidence.

Even when officers have had warrants, their rights to search private premises have often been limited. In *Ybarra* v. *Illinois* (1979), the Court held that a warrant to search a tavern and the bartender did not give the police the right to search customers who happened to be in the bar at the same time. In *Steagald* v. *United States* (1981), the Court ruled that an arrest warrant for one man did not allow officers to search for him in another man's house.

In other decisions, however, the Court has made law enforcement easier by allowing warrantless searches under certain circumstances. A warrantless search has always been possible if consent is given voluntarily. The Supreme Court has ruled that such permission does not necessarily have to come from the suspect. It may be given by an employee, a parent, or a friend who lives with the suspect.

Another exception to the warrant requirement is known as "hot pursuit." In one case, for example, police officers searching for an armed robber were directed to the house of a suspect immediately after the crime. During the course of the arrest, the officers searched the house and found a shotgun and a pistol. The Court ruled that the search was lawful because the police had to act quickly to protect themselves.

A third exception to the warrant requirement is called "plain view." The Court has held that if an officer stumbles across something incriminating that is in plain sight, it can be seized without a warrant and used as evidence. However, the officer must have a legal right to be on the premises, and the incriminating object must be "immediately apparent."

Another decision involving the search of premises went back to the *Boyd* case of 1886. This case had closely linked the Fourth Amendment to the Fifth. The case of *Andresen* v. *Maryland* (1976) grew out of records that had been seized—with a warrant—from a law office and a real-estate firm. The defendant claimed that seizing the records had violated his Fifth Amendment rights. The Supreme Court held that *forcing* the defendant to produce the papers would have led to self-incrimination. But taking them by means of a valid warrant did not and was therefore constitutional.

Limits on Possessions

If our homes are relatively safe from invasion, what about our possessions? It all depends. One of the guidelines followed by the Supreme Court is known as the "expectation of privacy." It is reasonable for us to expect privacy in our homes. But the things we own do not necessarily have the same protection.

Bank records provide a good example of this. In a 1976 decision, *United States* v. *Miller*, the Court ruled on an individual's checks and deposit slips that had been subpoenaed (officially requested) from a bank. Had these records been seized illegally? No, said the Court:

> The depositor takes the risk, in revealing his affairs to another, that the information will be conveyed by that person to the Government. . . . The Fourth Amendment does not prohibit the obtaining of information revealed to a third party and conveyed by him to the government.

A federal Drug Enforcement agent (left) and the Los Angeles police chief look over the cash and cocaine seized in a warehouse. The 20 tons of cocaine seized were estimated to have a street value of about $6.7 billion.

How about luggage? Here the Court has been stricter. One case, *United States* v. *Chadwick*, was decided in 1977. Agents in Boston were tipped off by the San Diego police that a padlocked footlocker accompanying Gregory Machado and Bridget Leary might contain narcotics. When the two travelers arrived in Boston by train, they were taken into police custody. Some time later, the Boston police opened the trunk and found drugs. The Supreme Court ruled that the search had been illegal.

> By placing personal effects inside a double-locked footlocker, respondents [Machado and Leary] manifested an expectation that the contents would remain free from public examination. No less than one who locks the doors of his home against intruders, one who safeguards his personal possessions in this manner is due the protection of the Warrant Clause.

In other words, Machado and Leary had a reasonable expectation of privacy. And certainly the officers had had time to obtain a warrant. The Supreme Court has made it clear that if the police have time to get a warrant, they should do so.

Even garbage has come to the Court's attention. The trash in question belonged—or had belonged—to Billy Greenwood, of Laguna Beach, California. Acting on a tip that he was dealing drugs, a local police officer had Greenwood's garbage seized. It contained cocaine and hashish. Greenwood was tried and convicted of drug possession. A California court overturned the conviction. But the Supreme Court reversed the state's decision in *California* v. *Greenwood* (1988). In the Court's opinion, Greenwood could not have had any reasonable expectation of privacy in regard to his garbage. "What a person knowingly exposes to the public," the Court said, "is not a subject of Fourth Amendment protection."

How Secure Are Our Persons?

The Los Angeles police were certain that Antonio Rochin was dealing drugs. In June 1949, they staged a raid on his house and surprised him in his bedroom. Agents spotted two tablets on a table. "Whose stuff is this?" they asked. At this point Rochin snatched up the tablets and swallowed them. The angry police stuck their fingers down Rochin's throat to try to get him to vomit. When this failed, they took him to a hospital and had his stomach pumped. The result was two morphine tablets. On the basis of this evidence, Rochin was tried, convicted, and sentenced to prison.

Justice Felix Frankfurter spoke for the Court in *Rochin* v. *California* (1952):

> [T]he proceedings by which this conviction was obtained do more than offend some fastidious squeamishness or private sentimental-ism about combatting crime too energetically. This is conduct that shocks the conscience.

The search had been illegal, the Court decided. It therefore reversed Rochin's conviction.

Later decisions indicated, however, that there are various degrees of bodily invasion. Not all of them are equally shocking. The Court's decision in *Breithaupt* v. *Abram* (1957) held that it was permissible to take a blood sample from an unconscious man who smelled of alcohol and had just been involved in a fatal auto accident. In *Cupp* v. *Murphy* (1973), the Court ruled that the police could forcibly take fingernail scrapings from a man. This evidence later helped convict him of murdering his wife.

On the other hand, the justices have taken a dim view of forced surgery to remove a bullet. The intended patient was a suspect in an armed robbery who had been shot by his victim. In *Winston* v. *Lee* (1985), the Supreme Court refused to allow the state of Virginia to carry out the 2½-hour operation. In the Court's opinion, this was too much of a "compelled surgical intrusion" into a person's body to be considered reasonable.

A new issue, drug testing on the job, arose during the late 1980s. So-called drug-free workplaces were the aim of both the government and private industry. In 1988, the federal government adopted regulations requiring random testing for 4 million people doing transportation-related work. Many private companies routinely test all job applicants. According to one estimate, about 8 million Americans were tested for drug use in 1989. This figure is expected to triple by 1992.

Several court cases have challenged drug testing. Most of them have done so on Fourth Amendment grounds. On the same day in 1989, the Supreme Court handed down decisions in two cases. One concerned railroad workers, the other employees of the U.S. Customs Service. (Neither of these cases involved random testing.)

The case of the railroad workers grew out of a rule requiring blood and urine tests of all crew members on any train involved in a serious accident. A lower court held that the requirement was unconstitutional because there was no probable cause or even reasonable suspicion involving any individual who had been tested. But the Supreme Court, in *Skinner* v. *Railway Labor Executives* (1989), upheld the regulation. Individual rights, said the Court, had to be balanced against the government's "compelling interest" in protecting the public.

As for customs workers, regulations require urine testing for all employees who carry firearms or handle drugs or classified material. After a federal court of appeals upheld the ruling, the Customs Service union appealed to the Supreme Court. The union also argued against testing that was not based on probable cause or reasonable suspicion. The Supreme Court upheld the decision of the lower court in *National Treasury Employees* v. *Von Raab* (1989). Drug testing of customs agents was justified because they are "the nation's first line of defense against one of the greatest problems affecting the health and welfare of our population."

Several justices dissented from these decisions. In the Customs Service case, Justice Antonin Scalia accused the government of using its own employees as a symbol for its opposition to drugs. "Symbolism," Scalia wrote, "even symbolism for so worthy a cause as the abolition of unlawful drugs, cannot validate an otherwise unreasonable search."

School Searches: A Special Category

In legal terms, schools are special places. School searches are also special. The main reason is that students—at least elementary and high school students—are minors, or juveniles. That is, they are under the age of eighteen. Since these students are not adults, their rights are not protected as fully as those of adults. Among other things, juveniles cannot vote or buy alcoholic beverages. Bill of Rights protections for minors are also limited. For instance, Supreme Court decisions have extended most of the rights of the accused to juvenile suspects. But the Court has also held that a minor does not have an adult's right to a jury trial in a serious criminal case.

Do the protections against unreasonable search and seizure provided by the Fourth Amendment apply to minors? Outside the school, these generally apply. In school, however, the story is different. Administrators, whose job is to maintain law and order, must prevent or punish such offenses as theft, assault, and drug use. In doing this, they can—and do—search students' lockers, desks, coats, handbags, and backpacks. In one instance, authorities looking for missing money conducted a strip search (one in which the person must undress) of an entire fifth-grade class. In another incident, administrators used marijuana-sniffing dogs to search all students of a junior and senior high school for illegal drugs.

Do actions like these violate students' rights? What protections do students have against unreasonable searches and seizures? Several court cases of the 1970s and early 1980s dealt with these questions at the levels of the state and lower federal courts. According to some of the decisions, students were protected by the Fourth Amendment. But other decisions held that Fourth Amendment guarantees did not apply. The reason usually given was that school officials stand *in loco parentis* (Latin for "in the place of a parent"). What this means in terms of search and seizure is that a school principal has as much right to search a student's locker as a mother has to look through her son's or daughter's closet.

This issue finally reached the Supreme Court in the case of *New Jersey* v. *T.L.O.* (1985). Here is what happened: One day in 1980, a teacher caught a fourteen-year-old high school freshman known as T.L.O. smoking in a school lavatory. (Her real name has never been released to the public.) When T.L.O. was taken before the school authorities, she denied the charge. In fact, she said, she didn't even smoke. An assistant principal searched her purse and found a pack of cigarettes. He then went on to find marijuana, rolling papers, and lists. All of these items seemed to indicate that T.L.O. was dealing drugs. She was suspended from school. She protested on the basis that the search had violated her constitutional rights.

The New Jersey Supreme Court ruled on the case as follows: (1) Students are protected by the Fourth Amendment. (2) School officials have the right to conduct searches of students without a warrant. (3) These officials must have "reasonable grounds" to believe that a student has shown evidence of illegal or disruptive behavior. (4) In the case of T.L.O., the search was *not* reasonable because the contents of her purse had no bearing on the charge against her. (Mere possession of cigarettes did not violate school rules.)

The U.S. Supreme Court agreed with the New Jersey Supreme Court on the first three points, but not on the fourth. Yes, juveniles are protected by Fourth Amendment guarantees, the Supreme Court said. But school officials do have a right to conduct warrant-less searches.

> Against the child's interest in privacy must be set the substantial interest of teachers and administrators in maintaining discipline in the classroom and on school grounds.

Yes, said the Court, reasonable suspicions are sometimes enough to justify a search without a warrant. In ordinary circumstances, authorities could carry out such a search only if they had probable cause to believe that a violation of the law had occurred. But the school setting "requires some modification of the level of suspicion of illicit activity needed to justify a search."

On the final point—the reasonableness of the search in the case of T.L.O.—the U.S. Supreme Court reversed the decision of the New Jersey Supreme Court. It held that the assistant principal was justified in beginning the search because he was looking for evidence to support the teacher's claim against T.L.O. Once it had been started, the search revealed damaging evidence that justified continuing it.

The *T.L.O.* decision left several questions unanswered, however. For one thing, it did not deal with the issue of locker and desk searches. Nor did it state whether the exclusionary rule applies to school searches. Most important, perhaps, it offered no guidelines for mass searches, such as those of the entire fifth-grade class and the junior and senior high schools.

CHAPTER 6

Search and Seizure: In Transit

"They told me many pretty things. That life here was easier, and so I came."

MEXICAN IMMIGRANT RUBEN V. [quoted in *To The Promised Land*]

Alexis de Tocqueville, the Frenchman who wrote the following words, visited the United States more than 150 years ago.

In the United States a man builds a house in which to spend his old age, and he sells it before the roof is on; he plants a garden and lets [rents] it just as the trees are coming into bearing; he brings a field into tillage [prepares it for planting crops] and leaves other men to gather the crops; he embraces a profession and gives it up; he settles in a place, which he soon afterwards leaves to carry his changeable longings elsewhere.

Tocqueville's observations about "Why the Americans Are So Restless in the Midst of Their Prosperity" still make sense. Americans are among the most mobile people on earth. In Tocqueville's time, horses, wagons, and steamboats carried them from the Atlantic Coast to the vast frontier of the West. Today they move from the frostbelt to the sunbelt by car, train, and plane. One recent survey showed that 17 percent of the population had moved at least once during the past twelve months.

A helicopter searches for marijuana. Several Supreme Court rulings in the late 1980s allowed such aerial surveillance.

Our "changeable longings" keep us on the go. Little wonder, then, that recent interpretations of the Fourth Amendment show that Americans are always in transit—always moving about.

A Nation on Wheels

When the U.S. Supreme Court handed down its decision in *Carroll* v. *United States* (1925), there were about 17 million cars on the nation's roads. Today there are 140 million. Since 1925, automobiles have spawned an immense highway network, created suburbs, and helped destroy inner cities. They have given us the motel, the billboard, the drive-in restaurant, and the shopping mall. They have also been used to commit crimes. Since *Mapp* v. *Ohio* made the Fourth Amendment applicable to state actions in 1961, cars have played a role in a growing number of Supreme Court cases.

The *Carroll* decision established what became known as the automobile exception. It held that searching a moving vehicle without a warrant was legal if the police could show probable cause. The *Carroll* precedent was affected somewhat by the Supreme Court's decision in *Terry* v. *Ohio* (1968). In this case, the Court ruled that probable cause was not necessary for a stop and frisk if a law officer believed the suspect was dangerous.

Many recent Supreme Court decisions involving automobiles have tended to relax earlier search-and-seizure guidelines. A case in point was *Adams* v. *Williams*, decided in 1972. A Connecticut patrolman named Connolly got a tip from someone he thought was reliable. According to this person—called an informant—Robert Williams was carrying a weapon. While he was on patrol, Connolly stopped Williams's car and asked him to open the door. When Williams did so, Connolly saw that there was a revolver tucked into his waistband. Further search of the car turned up heroin, a machete, and a second revolver.

After he was convicted, Williams claimed that the search was unreasonable because it went beyond the precedent set by the *Terry* case. The patrolman had acted only on an informant's tip, not on his own observations. The Supreme Court, however, decided that Connolly had acted properly.

The Fourth Amendment does not require a policeman who lacks the precise level of information necessary for probable cause to arrest to simply shrug his shoulders and allow a crime to occur or a criminal to escape.

Later cases continued to make automobile stop-and-frisk operations easier. *Michigan* v. *Long* (1983) began with an automobile that had been seen speeding and weaving down the highway. When deputies stopped the car, the driver, David Long, got out. Although a roadside frisk revealed no weapons, a search of Long's car turned up marijuana. The Court ruled that the frisk was permissible. "Roadside encounters between the police and suspects are especially hazardous," it said. Long might have returned to his car and gotten a gun if he had not been searched.

In *United States* v. *Hensley* (1985), the crucial factor was a "Wanted" flyer. Tipped off by this, an officer stopped Thomas Hensley, searched his car, and found two revolvers. Even this kind of stop and frisk was permissible, said the Supreme Court. The officer had to act quickly because the suspect might otherwise have escaped.

Clearly, when officers stop and frisk a driver, the contents of the car may also become part of the search. Here, too, recent Supreme Court rulings have tended to give law-enforcement agents the benefit of the doubt. In general, for instance, the Court has held that if the police have legally taken control of a vehicle, they do not need a search warrant in order to examine what is inside it. This is true even if such contents include closed luggage or other containers. In *United States* v. *Ross* (1982), the Court compared the search of a car with the search of a house:

When a legitimate search is under way, and when its purpose and its limits have been properly defined, nice [precise] distinctions

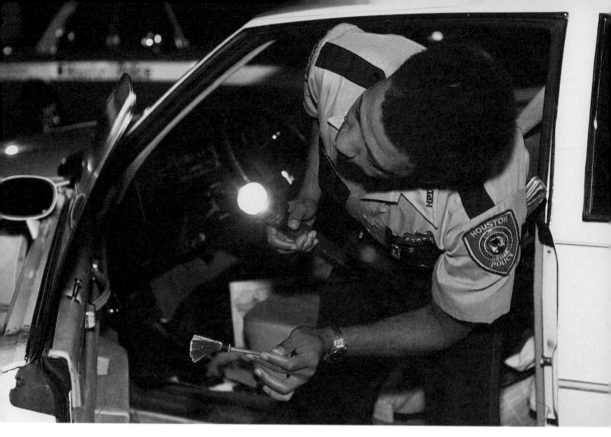

A Houston police officer searches a car for evidence.

between closets, drawers, and containers, in the case of a home, or between glove compartments, upholstered seats, trunks, and wrapped packages, in the case of a vehicle, must give way to the interest in the prompt and efficient completion of the task at hand.

In a 1990 case, *Alabama* v. *White*, warrantless searches were further broadened. Police in Montgomery, Alabama, received an anonymous tip about a woman named Vanessa White. She would be leaving a particular apartment at a particular time in a particular car on her way to a particular motel. Also, said the unnamed informant, she would have cocaine inside a brown briefcase. The police followed White, stopped her, and searched the car. They found a brown briefcase with marijuana. After White was arrested, the police found cocaine inside her purse. She was convicted of possessing drugs. White appealed on the basis of the exclusionary rule. But the Supreme Court upheld the conviction. The *White* case set a new precedent: An anonymous tip, if confirmed by independent police work, is reliable enough to justify an investigative search.

Another 1990 Supreme Court decision dealt with the question of whether highway police can set up a fixed checkpoint on a highway to check for drunk drivers. In *Michigan Department of State Police* v. *Sitz*, the Court upheld highway checkpoints for drunkenness— even though there was no probable cause to stop drivers. *All* vehicles passing through the checkpoint were stopped. Each driver was very briefly checked for signs of drunkenness. The Court said such a "stop" was a seizure in the Fourth Amendment sense. But it ruled that the measure of intrusion was slight compared with the state's "grave [serious] and legitimate" interest in preventing drunk driving.

Cars, Borders, and Illegal Immigrants

We have our lands, pure rocks. They don't produce anything. Crops barely grow. We have to go to the U.S. to have something better for our families.

Carlos R.—his last name is not revealed—comes from Mexico. Like thousands of others from his country, he entered the United States by crossing the border between the two countries illegally. Carlos R. and others like him are known as undocumented, or illegal, aliens. (An alien is someone who is not a citizen of the country in which he or she lives.) Illegal aliens come not just from Mexico. They also arrive from Central America, the Caribbean islands, Europe, and Asia. Obviously it's very hard to know how many illegal aliens there are in the United States. According to one estimate, about half a million enter the country every year.

The United States, like other nations, has the power to inspect people and goods that cross its borders. It does this routinely, even if there is no special cause for suspicion. U.S. immigration laws are administered by the Immigration and Naturalization Service (INS) and enforced by its uniformed branch, the Border Patrol. The INS

Undocumented aliens near the Mexican border.

is authorized to stop illegal aliens at the border, search for them elsewhere, and deport them—that is, send them home.

As early as 1896, the Supreme Court ruled that everyone in the United States is entitled to due process of law, as guaranteed by the Fourteenth Amendment. In 1982, the Court extended this protection specifically to undocumented aliens. At this time, one justice suggested that illegal aliens might even be entitled to special protection. Although they are encouraged by some employers to remain in this country because they provide cheap labor, illegal aliens are "nevertheless denied the benefits our society makes available to citizens and lawful residents."

Several cases involving illegal aliens have involved cars stopped at or near the border between the United States and Mexico. An early one, *Almeida-Sanchez* v. *United States*, was decided in 1973. The plaintiff, a Mexican citizen, had a valid work permit for the United States. He was subjected to a warrantless search (yielding marijuana) by a roving patrol. It stopped his car more than twenty miles from the border. The Court ruled that roving patrols cannot stop cars at this distance from the border without probable cause. "The *Carroll* doctrine does not declare a field day for the police in searching automobiles," said the Court's opinion. "Automobile or no automobile, there must be probable cause for a search."

Later cases have tended to relax search-and-seizure rules as they apply to undocumented aliens. A 1975 case began when Border Patrol police stopped a driver on a California road. He and his two passengers were found to be illegal aliens. The officers admitted that their only reason for stopping the car was that the three occupants "appeared to be of Mexican descent." In *United States* v. *Brignoni-Ponce* (1975), the Supreme Court ruled that this reason alone was not sufficient for stopping the car. The stop in this particular case was therefore illegal. But, the Court went on to say, a stop does *not* have to be justified by probable cause in cases involving illegal aliens. If an officer has a reasonable suspicion that a vehicle contains illegal aliens, he or she may stop it briefly and "investigate the circumstances that provoke suspicion."

Another case, *United States* v. *Martinez-Fuerte* (1976), concerned several different drivers who were stopped at two fixed checkpoints in California. All of the cars were found to be carrying illegal aliens from Mexico. At one of the checkpoints, cars that were not given the okay to go through were sent to a second inspection area. The defendants claimed that this process was unfair because all motorists were not treated equally. But the Court upheld what it called "selective referral." The stops were public and relatively routine. For this reason, the public should not find them "frightening or offensive." Besides, the Court said, selective referrals minimized inconvenience to the general public by focusing only on some cars. The Court found such referrals constitutional even if they were "made largely on the basis of apparent Mexican ancestry."

Justice William Brennan dissented from this decision. He said:

> Every American citizen of Mexican ancestry and every Mexican alien lawfully in this country must know after today's decision that he travels the fixed checkpoint highways at the risk of being subjected not only to a stop, but also to detention and interrogation, both prolonged and to an extent far more than for non-Mexican appearing motorists. . . . That deep resentment will be stirred by a sense of unfair discrimination is not difficult to foresee.

Searches in Other Circumstances

Not all INS enforcement involves border patrols. Illegal aliens are illegal wherever they are, of course. A common type of search is the "factory survey" conducted at a business that is said to employ undocumented aliens.

A fairly typical scene took place at three garment factories in Los Angeles. Some INS agents stood at the factory exits. Others, armed and carrying walkie-talkies, moved through the buildings asking employees questions about their citizenship. Backed by their union, four of the workers brought a lawsuit against the INS. All of them were either citizens or legal aliens. They argued that their Fourth Amendment rights had been violated. In effect, they said, the entire work force had been seized during the investigation.

This case, *I.N.S.* v. *Delgado*, came before the Supreme Court in 1984. The majority of the justices held that employees' liberty had not been restrained by either physical force or show of authority. Therefore, seizure of the entire work force had not taken place. The investigation was simply, in the words of the Court, a "classic consensual encounter"—a standard exchange governed by agreement. (Again, Justice Brennan denounced the Court's actions in a strongly worded dissent.)

Clearly, INS enforcement does not always involve border patrols. Likewise, border patrols do not always involve automobiles. Vast quantities of drugs and thousands of illegal immigrants enter the United States by boat every year. Long ago, Congress gave government officials permission to board ships whenever necessary.

Was this federal law in keeping with Fourth Amendment guarantees? No, said the owners of a 40-foot sailboat (registered in France) that was stopped near New Orleans in 1980. The 6,000 pounds of marijuana stored on board led to the owners being convicted under U.S. drug laws. The defendants insisted, however, that the search had been illegal. Officials had boarded the boat without "a reasonable suspicion of a law violation." This was required, after all, in highway searches.

The Supreme Court ruled otherwise in *United States* v. *Villamonte-Marquez* (1983). Boat traffic is very different from highway traffic, it said.

No reasonable claim can be made that permanent checkpoints would be practical on waters...where vessels can move in any direction at any time and need not follow established "avenues" as automobiles must do.

More important, though, is the matter of documents and the need to check them, said the Court. Shipping regulations govern such trades as fishing and towing. They control the movement of dangerous chemicals and weapons. They also prohibit the transport of illegal drugs, weapons, and persons.

While inspection of a vessel's documents might not always conclusively establish compliance with United States shipping laws, more often than not it will. While the need to make document checks is great, the resultant intrusion on Fourth Amendment interests is quite limited.

In 1989, the government began its Zero Tolerance Program. Now boats anywhere in coastal waters are subject to search. If any drugs are found on board, even among passengers, the vessels may be seized. The Coast Guard needs no search warrants, no probable cause, and not even reasonable suspicion to search a vessel.

Air Travel

In 1972, an unusual trial was held in a federal appeals court in New York City. It took place behind closed doors, a rare event in a democracy. In fact, the court itself spoke of secret proceedings as "odious," or hateful. At issue in the case of *United States* v. *Bell* (1972) was the "hijacker profile." (A profile is a list of characteristics and behaviors that are thought to be typical of a certain kind of person—in this case, an airplane hijacker.)

Hijacking became a threat as air travel increased after World War II. Hijackers are usually terrorists who call attention to their cause through violence and intimidation. Hijackers take control of a plane while it is in flight, usually at gunpoint. They force the pilot to land where they wish. Then, with the passengers as hostages, they try to get ransom or some other demand.

Early efforts to end hijacking focused on the hijacker profile. If passengers seemed to fit the description, security officials checked their papers and baggage with extra care. Obviously, officials did not want the public to know just what characteristics they were looking for. So when use of the profile became a Fourth Amendment issue, law-enforcement officials tried to keep them secret. They were successful in *United States* v. *Bell* (1971). The court upheld the use of a hijacker profile, saying that it did not violate Fourth Amendment guarantees.

The hijacker profile has not been used much in recent years, however. Instead, airports rely on electronic devices to detect weapons or explosives. All passengers must go through a metal detector called a magnetometer. Their carry-on baggage is viewed through an X-ray machine. If either of these devices indicates a problem, further checks are made. Legally, these "searches" are regarded as fair because all passengers are treated equally. Also, people are willing to undergo such checks because they think that doing so is a small price to pay to ensure everybody's safety.

While the hijacker profile may be out of favor, another profile has attracted attention. This is the drug-courier profile, a set of characteristics that officals believe indicate that someone may be carrying narcotics. In the beginning, the Supreme Court seemed to take a negative view of this method. At least it did so in an early case, *Reid* v. *Georgia* (1980). Tommy Reid, Jr., had been arrested at the Atlanta airport and later convicted of cocaine possession. He argued that his seizure had been unlawful because of the vagueness of the profile. The agent had regarded the following circumstances in Reid's case as suspicious: (1) He had come from Fort Lauderdale, Florida, where a lot of cocaine is sold. (2) He had arrived early in the morning, when drug enforcement is light. (3) He carried only a shoulder bag. (4) He seemed to be traveling with someone else, but trying to conceal the fact.

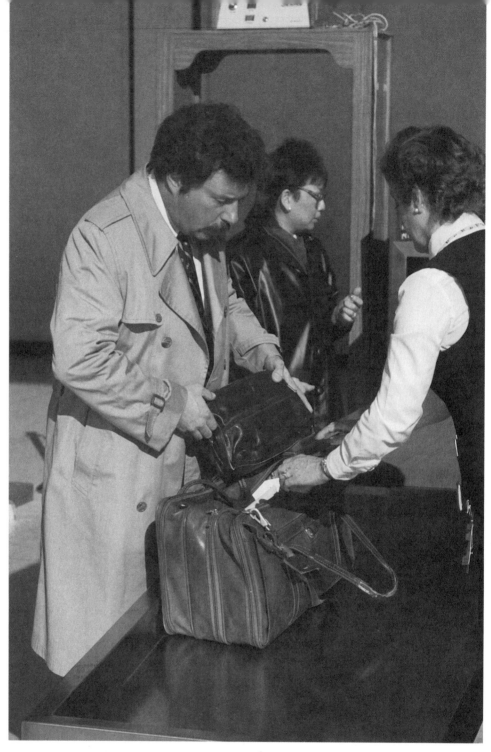

Airplane passengers walk through metal detector units while the contents of their carry-on luggage are viewed through x-ray machines. Such electronic devices are used to detect guns, bombs, and other possibly dangerous items that might be smuggled on board.

The Supreme Court agreed with Reid. It said characteristics (1) through (3) describe "a very large category of presumably innocent travelers." The only thing that set Reid apart was "the agent's belief that [Reid] and his companion were attempting to conceal the fact that they were traveling together." This "hunch," said the Court, was "simply too slender a reed to support the seizure in this case."

By 1989, things had begun to look different, or at least the profile did. For Andrew Sokolow, who was arrested in Hawaii with cocaine, the following circumstances were critical: He had traveled round-trip from Honolulu to Miami in less than forty-eight hours. He had checked no luggage. He had paid for his ticket in $20 bills. He had given a false name to the airline agent. He had also looked nervous. In the case of *United States* v. *Sokolow*, the Supreme Court declared:

> Any one of these factors is not by itself proof of any illegal conduct and is quite consistent with innocent travel. But we think taken together they amount to reasonable suspicion.

And "reasonable suspicion" is an adequate reason for the kinds of airport searches the courts call "investigatory stops."

Justice Thurgood Marshall dissented. He made this point, among others:

> Nothing about the characteristics shown by airport traveler Sokolow reasonably suggests that criminal activity is afoot. The majority's hasty conclusion to the contrary serves only to indicate its willingness, when drug crimes or anti-drug policies are at issue, to give short shrift [little consideration] to constitutional rights.

It should be noted that the Court's opinion emphasized the experience and observations of enforcement agents rather than their reliance on a drug profile. In any case, said the Drug Enforcement

Administration, it no longer relies on a single set of characteristics because "there are too many variables."

Aerial Searches

Does the Fourth Amendment protect homes, grounds, and similar property from aerial surveillance (observation from aircraft)? In general, said the Supreme Court majority, it does not. Decisions handed down in two cases in 1986 have provided some guidelines. In the first one, *California* v. *Ciraolo*, a privately grown patch of marijuana was protected from view on the ground by fences. Police officers, however, flew overhead. They were able to identify the plants from 1,000 feet in the air. They then got a search warrant that eventually led to Ciraolo's conviction on drug charges. The Court upheld his conviction. Ciraolo could have had no reasonable expectation of privacy, said the Court. "Any member of the public flying in this airspace who glanced down could have seen everything that these officers observed."

The second case, *Dow Chemical Company* v. *United States* (1986), involved the Environmental Protection Agency (EPA). The EPA had used aerial photographs, taken above a Dow plant in Michigan, to gather information on air pollution. Again, the Supreme Court held that such flights did not violate the Fourth Amendment. (As it turned out, the EPA and Dow reached a settlement without using the pictures.)

In both the *Ciraolo* and *Dow Chemical* cases, Justice Lewis Powell wrote dissenting opinions. Regarding *Ciraolo*, Powell said: "It would appear that, after today, families can expect to be free of official surveillance only when they retreat beyond the walls of their homes." He went on to add that the Court's approach "will not protect Fourth Amendment rights, but rather will permit their gradual decay as technology advances."

In both of these cases, surveillance had been carried out from aircraft flying fairly high. What about low-flying helicopters? The Court approved such searches in *Florida* v. *Riley* (1989). Marijuana observed from a helicopter flying at 400 feet was no more protected than marijuana seen from 1,000 feet, the Court said.

It is of obvious importance that the helicopter in this case was *not* violating the law, and there is nothing in the record or before us to suggest that helicopters flying at 400 feet are sufficiently rare in this country to lend substance to [Riley's] claim that he reasonably anticipated that his greenhouse would not be subject to observation from that altitude.

In other words, Riley, like Ciraolo, had no right to expect privacy for his grounds and his forbidden crop.

The Special Case of Electronic Surveillance

"The Fourth Amendment protects people, not places."

JUSTICE POTTER STEWART, in *Katz* v. *United States* (1967)

The complete story will not be revealed until the year 2027. Only then can the National Archives in Washington, D.C., unseal some extraordinary records. These are the tapes and transcripts made by the FBI when it conducted its electronic surveillance of the great civil rights leader Martin Luther King, Jr.

Quite a bit is known already, however. Congressional hearings of the 1970s showed the extent of the FBI's surveillance of King. Also, though many of the King tapes are sealed, others—resulting from investigations of his associates—have been made available.

Wiretaps were used on King's home and office telephones from late 1963 until the middle of 1966. In addition, "bugs" (concealed microphones) were installed in many of the hotel rooms where King stayed as he traveled around the United States. Transcripts of wiretapped and bugged conversations were circulated among FBI agents and shown to the attorney general. They even reached the president's desk. Some were offered to journalists, and published details of King's private life were used to try to discredit him.

This business office is undergoing a check for illegally placed electronic listening devices. Rival companies sometimes resort to industrial or business spying to gain a competitive edge over their competitors.

Why was the surveillance carried out? One reason, according to the FBI, was the bureau's fear of Communist influence on King and an organization he headed, the Southern Christian Leadership Conference. Another was concern about urban disorders, especially in African-American ghettos. (The Watts area of Los Angeles exploded in violence in 1965, and the following summer there were more than forty riots across the country.) Underlying these worries, however, was the deep hostility of FBI administrators toward King and the civil rights movement. An FBI report, for example, spoke of the "desired results" of the surveillance. One of these was "neutralizing King as an effective Negro leader"—that is, making him powerless. Another goal was "developing evidence concerning King's continued dependence on Communists for guidance and direction." At a press conference, FBI director J. Edgar Hoover called King "one of the lowest characters in the country" and "the most notorious liar in America."

During the 1960s, FBI electronic surveillance invaded the privacy of thousands of Americans. Some, like King, were public figures. (Among them were Paul Newman and Muhammad Ali.) Others were suspected of criminal activities. Many were ordinary citizens whose only "crime" was that they had criticized the U.S. government—or the FBI. Most of the victims did not know what was happening. King and his associates eventually found out, however. One of them said: "We knew they were bugging our phones but that was never really a problem for us. . . . In our conduct of a nonviolent movement there was nothing that we did not want them to know anyway."

Years of Uncertainty

How could the FBI get away with such widespread invasions of privacy? Didn't this surveillance violate the Fourth Amendment? In the case of the wiretaps on King, the bureau had the approval of the attorney general. It also operated under a presidential order of 1940, signed on the eve of World War II. This authorized wiretapping to protect "national security."

In the mid-1960s, the home and office telephones of Martin Luther King, Jr., were wiretapped. Concealed microphones were also placed in hotel rooms where he stayed when he traveled. Later, in an unrelated case decided in 1967, the Supreme Court ruled that warrantless electronic eavesdropping is an illegal search and seizure under most circumstances.

In any event, the legal standing of electronic surveillance during this period was uncertain. The *Olmstead* case of 1928 (Chapter 3) had declared that wiretapping was not covered by the Fourth Amendment. The amendment, the Court ruled, applied only to the physical invasion of property in search of a person or of "tangible effects" (material objects). But the *Olmstead* decision had also said that Congress could regulate wiretapping. Six years later, Congress passed the Federal Communications Act. It did not mention wiretapping as such, but it did include this provision: "No person not being authorized by the sender shall intercept any communication and divulge [reveal] or publish the existence, contents, substance, purport, effect or meaning of such intercepted communication to any person." In the case of *Nardone* v. *United States* (1937), the Supreme Court held that "intercepted communication" did indeed apply to wiretapping.

Did this federal law eliminate electronic surveillance? Not at all, for at least three reasons: (1) Many local and state police continued to use the technique. And evidence gained by wiretapping could be used at the state level until the *Mapp* decision in 1961. (2) The 1934 law applied only to wiretapping, not bugging. Concealed microphones, however, became possible with the invention of the transistor during the late 1940s. (3) Federal agencies interpreted the 1934 law to mean that agents could *intercept* communications as long as they did not *divulge* them. According to this view, even federal wiretapping and bugging operations were legal as long as the results were not made public.

Electronic surveillance therefore went on all the time. When cases involving it did reach the Supreme Court, the Court continued to apply the *Olmstead* rule. It held that as long as there was no physical invasion of premises for actual things, the Fourth Amendment did not apply.

The *Katz* Landmark and a New Law

Charles Katz was a bookmaker, or bookie. For a fee, he took bets and paid off the winners. Los Angeles was his home, but he often dealt with bettors who were as far away as Miami and Boston. This was strictly against federal law, and the FBI got on his trail.

Katz often kept in touch with his clients through a phone in a particular public booth. FBI agents attached a bug to the outside of the booth. Several incriminating phone calls were recorded. These helped convict Katz in a California court. He appealed. Katz argued that his privacy had been invaded and his Fourth Amendment rights violated. The Supreme Court agreed. This landmark ruling of 1967 overturned the *Olmstead* decision.

The petitioner [Katz] has strenuously argued that the booth was a "constitutionally protected area." The Government [the prosecutors who brought Katz to trial] has maintained with equal vigor that it was not. But this effort to decide whether or not a given "area," viewed in the abstract, is "constitutionally protected" deflects [turns away] attention from the problem presented by this case. For the Fourth Amendment protects people, not places. What a person knowingly exposes to the public, even in his own home or office, is not a subject of Fourth Amendment protection. . . . But what he seeks to preserve as private, even in an area accessible [open] to the public, may be constitutionally protected.

In effect, said the Court, spoken words *are* protected by the Fourth Amendment. This is so whether or not there is actual physical intrusion into premises.

In the case of *Katz* v. *United States* (1967), Justice John Marshall Harlan wrote an important concurring opinion. (A concurring opinion is one that agrees with the majority opinion but for different or additional reasons.) It was this case that prompted Harlan to define the concept of a reasonable "expectation of privacy" discussed in Chapters 5 and 6. Katz acted with this expectation. Although a phone booth is public, said Harlan, "it is a temporarily private place whose momentary occupants' expectations of freedom from intrusion are recognized as reasonable."

Like the *Olmstead* case thirty-nine years earlier, the *Katz* decision led to a new law governing electronic surveillance. This happened because of an additional point made by the Court. Since electronic surveillance *was* a form of search and seizure, it could be made reasonable if certain safeguards were followed. Congress now spelled out these safeguards. The new regulations formed Title III of the Omnibus Crime Control and Safe Streets Act of 1968. ("Title," used in this way, means a section of a law.)

Title III, which covered bugging as well as wiretapping, had several provisions. To carry out surveillance, a law-enforcement agency had to get a warrant in advance. This had to show probable cause that a crime had occurred and that the target of the surveillance was involved. The surveillance could deal only with certain crimes that were listed. They included murder, kidnapping, robbery, bribery, and drug dealing.

Ironically, the Nixon administration, the very one that had urged passage of the 1968 Omnibus Crime Act, itself fell victim to electronic surveillance. Nixon was disgraced by the scandal known as Watergate. It began in 1972, when Nixon was running for a second term. Men hired by a private organization, the Committee to Re-elect the President, tried to wiretap phones at the offices of

Democratic National Committee. The scandal unfolded through tape recordings of Nixon's conversations made with his knowledge. The Watergate scandal ended in 1974 when the president resigned. He was the first president in the nation's history to resign from office.

Wonderworld and Wiretapping

The time: November 1982. The scene: a Chicago courtroom. The cast was dominated by a sick but feisty defendant named Roy Williams. The real star of the show, however, was a series of taped conversations. These tapes were so riveting that the judge liked to refer to the chief prosecutor as Cecil B. deMille, the legendary Hollywood director.

The case in question pitted the Justice Department against the Teamsters Union, which has been found to have links with organized crime. The defendants were Williams, president of the union, and four of his associates. They were accused of trying to bribe Senator Howard Cannon of Nevada to sidetrack a trucking deregulation bill. The Teamsters opposed the bill because it threatened to allow many new companies to enter the business and therefore undercut union wages.

The bribe offered was nothing so simple as a cash payment or a political contribution. Instead, it was a chance to buy a piece of real estate, known as Wonderworld, in Las Vegas, Nevada. The land, next to some owned by Cannon, was owned but not directly controlled by the Teamsters' pension fund. It was valued at $1.6 million. Teamsters officials promised it to Cannon for $1.4 million in return for his help in sidetracking the deregulation bill. As it turned out, the deal fell through and Cannon did not buy the land. He later supported the deregulation bill and was never indicted, or charged.

This outcome, however, did not affect the case against the Teamsters. The government believed, and was determined to prove, that they had attempted bribery. To build its case, the Justice Department obtained the necessary warrants under Title III of the Omnibus Crime Control Act. It then installed phone taps and bugs in the office of Allen Dorfman, a close associate and co-defendant of Williams. (For this reason, the case is titled *United States* v. *Dorfman*.)

Beginning early in 1979 and continuing for fourteen months, listening devices recorded about 2,000 reels of conversations. Most of them are filled with obscenities. The trial jury of six men and six women heard about fifty-five hours' worth of tapes, via stereophonic speakers, while the defendants sat glumly staring at the ceiling.

One of the most damaging tapes was recorded in Dorfman's office on May 21. Against background sounds of a groaning office chair and clinking ice cubes, three men had a conversation. They were Dorfman himself and two of his employees, William Webbe and Don Peters. The subject was a January 10 meeting in Cannon's Las Vegas office. Dorfman, Williams, and Cannon had discussed the bribe, while Webbe stood in the corridor outside.

DORFMAN: Well, the only bad part about the whole thing see if we had said to him [Cannon], well let's look into it, you know, because now it's really not under the custody and control of the fund anymore, and so on and so forth. But Roy Williams just unequivocally [clearly] came right out and says, you got the property Senator, don't worry about it. It's our property, you own it. You got a commitment from him [Williams].

WEBBE: You take care of your end.

DORFMAN: And I turned to Roy, cause he verified it the other day, I said Roy, we made a firm commitment to this guy. . . . And even when we were walking out of his office . . . you were standing there.

WEBBE: I was there.

DORFMAN: And, uh, you'll have everything, and he [Cannon] says and you fellows will take care of that property thing? Don't worry about it's all taken care of.

WEBBE: Roy said you take care of your end and we'll take care of our end for you.

DORFMAN: That's right.

Cannon and Williams, testifying at the trial, both denied that any attempted bribery had taken place. Even when Williams was shown a transcript of one of his own phone conversations, he claimed to remember nothing about it. "It's my language, it's my verbiage [words]," he said. "I've heard it played and it's my voice. But I have no personal knowledge of this telephone conversation."

Apparently the jury had trouble believing in such memory lapses. After listening for two months and deliberating for twenty-seven hours, the jury found all five defendants guilty. Five weeks later, Dorfman was killed in a gangland-style shooting in a Chicago suburb. Williams was later sentenced to a fifty-five-year prison term. But his sentence was canceled on condition that he resign his position as president of the Teamsters Union.

The *Williams* case showed how well wiretapping can work when it is properly undertaken and presented in court. The judge called it the "most significant" case in the history of electronic surveillance. In the words of Robert Blakey, who drafted Title III of the Omnibus Act, "This case represents a quantum leap [dramatic advance] forward in imagination and aggressiveness."

Recent Developments

In the world of electronics, the law always seems to be playing catch-up ball. When Title III was passed, it was believed to reflect the latest surveillance technology. But this law soon became outdated.

The 1968 law protected "aural" communications (those related to hearing) transmitted by wire and capable of being understood by the human ear. It did not deal with cellular telephones, which operate by radio signals. Nor did it cover electronic mail—messages sent between computers. These are easier targets for eavesdropping than telephone conversations. Telephone companies do not record conversations. Electronic mail services, however, routinely keep backup copies of messages.

In 1986, Congress passed a new law, the Electronic Communication Privacy Act. This law stated that warrants are required for the interception of cellular telephone conversations. It also required warrants for investigations of electronic mail that was less than six months old. (Most people who use these services keep messages for only a few months.)

Again, however, there was a gap between what the law covered and what was going on in the real world. The law did not cover cordless telephones. It did not cover closed-circuit television cameras. It did not cover sensing devices that can be tracked by satellites high above the earth. It did not cover laser technology. A laser beam can pick up conversations from vibrations the spoken voice makes in windows. These can be read by computer and converted into sounds. There is undoubtedly other government technology that is being kept under the tightest security so that only a very few people know anything about it.

What's more, even the laws on the books cover only *government* surveillance. Private surveillance is illegal. But the materials for making wiretapping, bugging, and other devices are easy to get. They can also be put together quite easily. There is no doubt that they are being used.

In 1986, for instance, warrants were authorized for 673 electronic interceptions. Of these, 643 were actually installed. There is every reason to believe that this number represents only the tiny tip of a very large iceberg. Justice Brandeis's warnings in the *Olmstead* case more than sixty years ago (see Chapter 3) are still very much to the point.

The Pros and Cons of the Exclusionary Rule

"Only a nation that reveres its judges would permit them to bar illegally obtained evidence from use, regardless of its probity [trustworthiness]."

FRED P. GRAHAM, *The Self-Inflicted Wound*

Near the southern tip of Manhattan island is an old and crowded neighborhood known as the East Village. Less than a square mile in area, it is home to about 67,000 New Yorkers. They form a racial mix of Hispanics, whites, and blacks. Alongside its rundown apartment buildings, the area has its share of fine brownstones, boutiques, restaurants, and theaters. It is also known as a center for drug dealing.

During the mid-1980s, a law school professor named H. Richard Uviller got to know the East Village well. After teaching at New York City's Columbia University for several years, he had come to feel "somewhat out of it," as he later wrote in a book about his experiences. Uviller was especially interested in Supreme Court decisions that affected law enforcement. "I realized I no longer knew how the Court's message sounded in the stationhouse and the squad car," he wrote. He therefore arranged to spend eight months accompanying East Village police officers as they went about their hard and dangerous work.

Associate Justice William J. Brennan, Jr., served on the Supreme Court from 1956 to 1990. He was a strong supporter of the exclusionary rule, the rule that illegally obtained evidence cannot be used in trials.

Uviller was in on interrogations, lineups, and drug busts. He spent hours in the backseat of squad cars as officers patrolled the neighborhood. He also listened to the questions police asked him about the law. One topic of constant debate was searches and seizures. Officers were especially concerned about the exclusionary rule, the rule that makes illegally obtained evidence inadmissible in court. In his book, Uviller wrote:

> What did the police make of the Court's instructions? . . . While the cops I spoke with are not familiar with the tortuous evolution [complex changes] of doctrine, . . . they certainly appreciate the bare fact that the rule changes and that its various forms almost always provoke a division of votes on the Court. "How am I supposed to know what to do," Rocky Regina [one of the police officers] complained loudly, "when nine justices can't even agree about when I did wrong?"

It was a good question, and a hard one to answer. The exclusionary rule has been the subject of many cases and disputes since it first came into being.

Burger Speaks Out

The exclusionary rule was created by the *Weeks* case in 1914 (Chapter 2). But its impact wasn't really felt until after 1961. That was when *Mapp* (Chapter 4) made the rule applicable to state as well as federal trials: illegally obtained evidence could not be used in court.

During the early years after *Mapp*, most Supreme Court decisions stressed the importance of strict law-enforcement procedures. Only by following these could the evidence gathered by police and prosecutors be admitted in court. The trend was obvious in two cases of the 1960s. The first, *Aguilar* v. *Texas*, was decided in 1964. The second, *Spinelli* v. *United States*, came five years later. In both instances, search warrants had been issued after police received tips from anonymous informants. Lower courts had convicted the two accused, one for possession of drugs and the other for bookmaking. The Court reversed both decisions. It ruled that the search warrants had been improper because they did not contain enough information.

On the basis of these two cases, the Supreme Court worked out a "two-pronged test" for issuing a valid search warrant based on the testimony of an informant: (1) The warrant had to reveal the circumstances on which the informant based his or her conclusion. (2) The warrant had to provide enough information to make it clear that the informant was telling the truth.

Justice Hugo Black was among those who thought that matters had gone too far. In his dissent from the decision handed down in *Spinelli*, he voiced a complaint. It now seemed to him that the magistrate issuing the search warrant had to conduct practically "a full-fledged trial." Nothing in the Constitution, Black wrote, "requires that the facts be established with that degree of certainty and with such elaborate specificity [detail]."

But stronger words would soon come from the chief justice himself, Warren Burger. The case that provoked Burger has the lengthy title of *Bivens* v. *Six Unknown Federal Narcotics Agents*. Bivens's apartment had been ransacked by agents searching for narcotics. They had neither a search warrant nor an arrest warrant, and they found nothing. When Bivens sued the agents for damages, the lower court ruled against him on the grounds that he had no legal right to do so. (At this time, an individual could not bring a damage suit against federal officials.) The Supreme Court reversed this decision in 1971. It ruled that individuals *could* sue federal officials for damages.

Chief Justice Burger dissented. First of all, he said, the Court had no right to allow Bivens's suit for damages. There was no constitutional basis for it. The only way to prevent police abuses was the exclusionary rule. The Court had been insisting on this for more than fifty years. Burger thought this was a mistake. Now the *Bivens* case showed the "suppression doctrine," as Burger called the exclusionary rule, in its true light. "I do not question the need for some remedy to give meaning and teeth to the constitutional guarantees against unlawful conduct by government officials," he said. But the hope that this objective could be reached by excluding reliable evidence from criminal trials "was hardly more than a wistful dream." The *Bivens* case showed just how useless the exclusionary rule was. An unlawful act had been committed against someone who was apparently totally innocent (Bivens). Since there was no constitutional way to punish this injustice, the Supreme Court constructed "a remedy of its own."

One of the main problems with the exclusionary rule, said Burger, is that it has been applied so rigidly:

Chief Justice Warren E. Burger served on the Supreme Court from 1969 to 1986. He strongly opposed the exclusionary rule.

Inadvertent [unplanned] errors of judgment that do not work any grave injustice will inevitably occur under the pressure of police work. These honest mistakes have been treated in the same way as deliberate and flagrant [extreme]... violations of the Fourth Amendment.... Freeing either a tiger or a mouse in a schoolroom is an illegal act, but no rational person would suggest that these two acts be punished in the same way.

Burger did propose a possible substitute for the exclusionary rule. It will be discussed, along with other suggested remedies, in the final section of this chapter.

Narrowing the Scope

Chief Justice Burger was not alone. Other justices shared his opposition to the exclusionary rule. Many Supreme Court decisions during the Burger years (1969 to 1986) limited its use. The case of *United States* v. *Janis* is one example. In this 1976 case, the Court refused to apply the exclusionary rule to evidence that had been seized illegally in a federal tax proceeding. Doing so would have meant extending the rule to a civil action. Normally, of course, Fourth Amendment protections apply only to criminal cases.

Another example is *Stone* v. *Powell*, also decided in 1976. Here, too, the Court ruled against the accused. Burger, this time in a concurring opinion, took advantage of the case to attack the exclusionary rule once more:

In *Weeks*, the Court emphasized that the Government, under settled principles of common law, had no right to keep a person's *private* papers. The Court noted that the case did not involve "burglar's tools or other *proofs of guilt....*" From this origin, the exclusionary rule has been changed in focus entirely. It is now used almost exclusively to exclude from evidence articles which are unlawful to be possessed or tools and instruments of crime. Unless it can be rationally thought that the Framers considered it essential to protect the liberties of the people to hold that which it is unlawful to possess, then it becomes clear that our constitutional course has taken a most bizarre tack [weird direction].

The case of *Illinois* v. *Gates* (1983) grew out of an unsigned letter to the police of Bloomingdale, Illinois. It read in part:

> This letter is to inform you that you have a couple in your town who strictly make their living on selling drugs. They are Sue and Lance Gates, they live on Greenway, off Bloomingdale Rd. in the condominiums. Most of their buys are done in Florida. Sue his wife drives their car to Florida, where she leaves it to be loaded up with drugs, then Lance flys [flies] down and drives it back. . . . May 3 she is driving down there again and Lance will be flying down in a few days to drive it back. . . . Presently they have over $100,000 worth of drugs in their basement. They brag about the fact they never have to work, and make their entire living on pushers.

Surveillance by the police indicated that the letter writer knew what he or she was talking about. So they got a search warrant. Acting on it, the police examined the Gateses' car and home. They found large amounts of drugs.

Lance and Sue Gates were convicted but asked for a Supreme Court review of the case. They argued that the search warrant failed to meet the two-pronged test for an informant's tip that had been set up by *Aguilar* and *Spinelli*. The Court agreed. But instead of throwing out the evidence, the justices threw out the two-pronged rule. From now on, they said, a search warrant based on an informant's tip would be valid on the basis of the "totality of circumstances." If all the police statements taken together were convincing, then a magistrate, using "practical common sense," would have probable cause to issue a warrant.

In a concurring opinion, Justice Byron White wrote:

The trend and direction of our exclusionary rule decisions indicate not a lesser concern with safeguarding the Fourth Amendment but a fuller appreciation of the high costs incurred when . . . reliable evidence is barred because of investigative error.

Fears of "Slow Strangulation"

Two decisions of 1984 further limited the exclusionary rule. In *Nix* v. *Williams*, the Supreme Court clearly recognized a principle called "inevitable discovery." Simply put, this means that illegally seized evidence can be used in court if it would have been found anyway.

The case of *United States* v. *Leon* (1984) grew out of a faulty search warrant, one that had been issued without probable cause. The Supreme Court ruled, however, that this fact did not make the evidence obtained through the warrant unusable in court. In preparing their affidavit (sworn statement) for the magistrate, the police had not acted dishonestly or recklessly. Also, they did have "an objectively reasonable belief" that probable cause existed. Although an error had been made, excluding evidence was too harsh a penalty to pay. After all, the Court pointed out, the purpose of the exclusionary rule is to prevent police misconduct, not to punish magistrates' mistakes. The *Leon* case set a new standard—that of "good faith"—for deciding whether a search warrant is valid and therefore whether evidence has been legally obtained.

One justice, William Brennan, consistently opposed the decisions limiting the use of the exclusionary rule. In his dissent in the *Janis* case, Brennan spoke of the "slow strangulation of the exclusionary rule." He came back to this idea in his dissent in *Leon*:

In case after case, I have witnessed the Court's gradual but determined strangulation of the [exclusionary] rule. It now appears that the Court's victory over the Fourth Amendment is complete. . . . The Court seeks to justify on the ground that the "costs" of adhering to the exclusionary rule in cases like those before us exceed the "benefits."

Brennan accused the Court of exaggerating the costs of the exclusionary rule and minimizing its benefits:

> The majority ignores the fundamental constitutional importance of what is at stake here. While the machinery of law enforcement and indeed the nature of crime itself have changed dramatically since the Fourth Amendment became part of the nation's fundamental law in 1791, what the Framers understood then remains true today—that the task of combating crime and convicting the guilty will in every era seem of such critical and pressing concern that we may be lured by temptations of expediency [what seems needed] into forsaking our commitment to protecting individual liberty and privacy. It was for that very reason that the Framers of the Bill of Rights insisted that law enforcement efforts be permanently and unambiguously [clearly] restricted in order to preserve personal freedoms.

In 1990, Brennan found himself in the majority for a change. The case, *James* v. *Illinois*, grew out of a murder trial in Chicago. One exception to the exclusionary rule had long been allowed. Prosecutors could use illegally obtained evidence in order to discredit a defendant's testimony. In this case, defendant Darryl James did not take the stand. But the prosecution used illegally obtained evidence to throw doubt on the testimony of one of his witnesses.

This would not do, said the Supreme Court. In his majority opinion, Brennan wrote that "this expansion would vastly increase the number of occasions on which such evidence could be used." Not only that, but "it would also deter defendants from calling witnesses in the first place." He went on to say:

> So long as we are committed to protecting the people from the disregard of their constitutional rights during the course of criminal

investigations, inadmissibility of illegally obtained evidence must remain the rule, not the exception.

The decision in the *James* case was front-page news. It reaffirmed the exclusionary rule at a time when it was under strong pressure. For the time being at least, the basic principle seemed to be safe.

Does the Rule Work?

Both the Burgers and Brennans of the legal profession would agree on one thing: The basic purpose of the exclusionary rule is to police the police. In other words, it seeks to prevent law-enforcement agents from using unlawful searches and seizures in order to collect evidence. How well does the rule work?

Part of the answer to this question has to do with warrants. The exclusionary rule is meant to encourage the police to obtain search warrants. A search warrant, properly drawn up, is the best guarantee of reasonableness. But the majority of police operations do not involve warrants at all. San Francisco in 1968 offers a typical example. In that city of about 750,000 people and 30,000 reported crimes, exactly twenty search warrants were issued for the entire year. Two decades later, H. Richard Uviller found a similar situation in New York City. The police whom he observed hardly ever used warrants. According to one estimate, more than 90 percent of all police searches are warrantless.

Clearly, the exclusionary rule does not seem to encourage search warrants. There are other negatives, too. The rule works only in the small number of cases that go to court. About 90 percent of criminal cases end not in trials but in guilty pleas. Another problem is that the rule is no help for the innocent victim of an unreasonable search. Innocence, of course, means no trial, which means that the exclusionary rule does not come into play.

What about cases where the exclusionary rule does play a role? Does the public benefit from it? Or, as one of Uviller's police officers put it: Does it protect "the bad guys" while "the good guys are left out in the cold''? The results of studies on the question are not clear-cut. One done during the late 1960s found that the effects of the rule could not be measured in an objective way. But another, released by the General Accounting Office in 1979, was more definite. According to this GAO study, motions to suppress evidence—that is, attempts to keep evidence out—were filed by only one out of ten defendants. These motions were usually denied:

> Thus, evidence was excluded as a result of Fourth Amendment violations in only 1.3 percent of the cases. Moreover, prosecutions were dropped in less than one half of one percent of the cases because of search and seizure problems.

Another study, done by the Chicago *Tribune,* was released in 1985. Its conclusions were similar to those of the GAO. During a thirteen-month period, fewer than 1 percent of Chicago cases involving violent crimes were dismissed because of illegally seized evidence. In many cases when evidence was suppressed, the defendants were found guilty anyway.

The results of the GAO and *Tribune* studies indicate that the exclusionary rule seems to do little harm. How much good it accomplishes, though, is another matter.

Might there be a better way to police the police? In his *Bivens* dissent, Chief Justice Burger offered what he considered a ''meaningful alternative.'' He recommended that Congress provide for a special agency or court. It would hear cases in which citizens claimed that their Fourth Amendment rights had been violated. This special court could also award money damages if the police had indeed acted unlawfully.

Another expert in constitutional law, Anthony Amsterdam, has suggested a different approach. He believes that the police themselves should draw up regulations providing for reasonable searches and seizures. The rules would then be reviewed by the courts. Officers who broke these rules would be disciplined.

Still another technique, supported by Uviller, is the so-called California model. It relies on warrants but makes them much easier to obtain than they are at present in most states. A police officer can radio a warrant request at any time of the day or night. She or he is switched into a three-way hookup with a prosecutor and a judge. The officer, under oath, requests a warrant. The prosecutor states his or her position. Then the judge makes a decision. A tape records everything that is said, in case the request should be challenged in the future. If the warrant is granted, the officer fills in the blanks on a standard form and carries out the search. This method has been successful in San Diego County, California.

There are many unanswered questions about the exclusionary rule. One thing is fairly clear, however: Even the most outspoken opponents of the exclusionary rule do not want to abolish it unless a workable substitute can be found.

Congress of the United States

begun and held at the City of New-York, on

Wednesday the fourth of March, one thousand seven hundred and eighty nine.

THE Convention of a number of the States, having at the time of their adopting the Constitution, expressed a desire, in order to prevent misconstruction or abuse of its powers, that further declaratory and restrictive clauses should be added: And as extending the ground of public confidence in the Government, will best ensure the beneficent ends of its institution.

RESOLVED by the Senate and House of Representatives of the United States of America, in Congress assembled, two thirds of both Houses concurring, that the following Articles be proposed to the Legislatures of the several States, as amendments to the Constitution of the United States, all, or any of which Articles, when ratified by three fourths of the said Legislatures, to be valid to all intents and purposes, as part of the said Constitution; viz.

ARTICLES in addition to, and amendment of the Constitution of the United States of America, proposed by Congress, and ratified by the Legislatures of the several States, pursuant to the fifth Article of the original Constitution.

Article the first... After the first enumeration required by the first Article of the Constitution, there shall be one Representative for every thirty thousand, until the number shall amount to one hundred, after which, the proportion shall be so regulated by Congress, that there shall be not less than one hundred Representatives, nor less than one Representative for every forty thousand persons, until the number of Representatives shall amount to two hundred, after which the proportion shall be so regulated by Congress, that there shall not be less than two hundred Representatives, nor more than one Representative for every fifty thousand persons.

Article the second. No law, varying the compensation for the services of the Senators and Representatives, shall take effect, until an election of Representatives shall have intervened.

Article the third. Congress shall make no law respecting an establishment of religion, or prohibiting the free exercise thereof; or abridging the freedom of speech, or of the press, or the right of the people peaceably to assemble, and to petition the Government for a redress of grievances.

Article the fourth. A well regulated militia, being necessary to the security of a free State, the right of the people to keep and bear arms, shall not be infringed.

Article the fifth. No Soldier shall, in time of peace be quartered in any house, without the consent of the owner, nor in time of war, but in a manner to be prescribed by law.

Article the sixth. The right of the people to be secure in their persons, houses, papers, and effects, against unreasonable searches and seizures, shall not be violated, and no warrants shall issue, but upon probable cause, supported by oath or affirmation, and particularly describing the place to be searched, and the persons or things to be seized.

Article the seventh. No person shall be held to answer for a capital, or otherwise infamous crime, unless on a presentment or indictment of a Grand Jury, except in cases arising in the land or naval forces, or in the militia, when in actual service in time of War or public danger; nor shall any person be subject for the same offence to be twice put in jeopardy of life or limb; nor shall be compelled in any criminal case to be a witness against himself, nor be deprived of life, liberty, or property, without due process of law; nor shall private property be taken for public use without just compensation.

Article the eighth. In all criminal prosecutions, the accused shall enjoy the right to a speedy and public trial, by an impartial jury of the State and district wherein the crime shall have been committed, which district shall have been previously ascertained by law, and to be informed of the nature and cause of the accusation; to be confronted with the witnesses against him; to have compulsory process for obtaining witnesses in his favor, and to have the assistance of counsel for his defense.

Article the ninth. In suits at common law, where the value in controversy shall exceed twenty dollars, the right of trial by jury shall be preserved, and no fact tried by a jury shall be otherwise re-examined in any court of the United States, than according to the rules of the common law.

Article the tenth. Excessive bail shall not be required, nor excessive fines imposed, nor cruel and unusual punishments inflicted.

Article the eleventh. The enumeration in the Constitution, of certain rights, shall not be construed to deny or disparage others retained by the people.

Article the twelfth. The powers not delegated to the United States by the Constitution, nor prohibited by it to the States, are reserved to the States respectively, or to the people.

ATTEST,

Frederick Augustus Muhlenberg, Speaker of the House of Representatives.

John Adams, Vice-President of the United States, and President of the Senate.

John Beckley, Clerk of the House of Representatives.
Sam. A. Otis Secretary of the Senate.

Perspectives

"It is a fair summary of history to say that the safeguards of liberty have frequently been forged in controversies involving not very nice people."

Justice Felix Frankfurter, in *United States* v. *Rabinowitz* (1950)

On the subject of Fourth Amendment guarantees, a Supreme Court justice once wrote:

These . . . rights belong in the catalog of indispensable freedoms. Among deprivations of rights, none is so effective in cowing a population, crushing the spirit of the individual and putting terror in every heart. Uncontrolled search and seizure is one of the first and most effective weapons in the arsenal of every arbitrary government.

Robert Jackson wrote these words more than forty years ago. Few people would argue with them today. But many aspects of the law of search and seizure have led to disagreement. And, since the Fourth Amendment is a living part of the Constitution, it will no doubt continue to provoke passionate debate in the future.

On September 25, 1789, the Congress of the United States proposed twelve articles as amendments to the Constitution. Except for the first two, they were ratified by the required number of states by December 15, 1791. These ten amendments have since become known as the Bill of Rights.

A Look Back

Looking back, it may seem that the history of the Fourth Amendment is a confused jumble—just one Supreme Court case after another. (In a recent book, a noted expert calls his discussion of search and seizure "The Fourth Amendment Can of Worms.") The history of the Fourth Amendment makes more sense if we remember that this vital part of the Bill of Rights consists of a single sentence that became part of the U.S. Constitution 200 years ago.

Like other provisions of the Bill of Rights—indeed, like the Constitution as a whole—the Fourth Amendment is stated in broad, general terms. Take another look at the words of the amendment. From the beginning, they led to questions. What makes a search "unreasonable"? For that matter, what exactly is a search? As our country developed, we have relied on the courts to provide the answers to questions like these. The Supreme Court, our highest judicial body, has tried to do so in the hundreds of decisions and opinions it has handed down. No wonder President Woodrow Wilson spoke of the Court as "a constitutional convention in continuous session."

The courts have carried out their task of interpretation and explanation in a constantly changing nation. When the Bill of Rights became law, the United States had about 4 million people clustered mainly along the Atlantic coast. The majority of its citizens were descendants of white Protestants from the British Isles. Most of them were farmers who lived in rural areas. During the next 200 years, the United States grew to a nation of more than 245 million people in a land that stretched to Hawaii and Alaska. Streams of immigrants had enriched its population. Most Americans lived in or near cities, working at the great variety of jobs necessary to maintain a modern industrial society.

A changing country was reflected in new laws and in new interpretations of older laws. Consider the Fourth Amendment alone. Within just a few decades, the Supreme Court has learned to

Chief Justice Earl Warren (seated, center) served on the Supreme Court from 1953 to 1959. During that time the Supreme Court was often referred to as the Warren Court. It handed down many decisions that expanded the rights of citizens. These included decisions extending protections such as the right of the accused to have illegally seized evidence excluded from trials.

deal with automobiles, telephones, airplanes, and helicopters, not to mention bootleg liquor, drugs, and illegal aliens.

Of course, the legal system of the United States does not deal only with changes in our physical environment. It also mirrors the ideals and hopes we have about our society. Again, consider the Fourth Amendment alone. Beginning in the 1960s, the United States witnessed an epidemic of crime and drug abuse. Supreme Court decisions upholding citizens' rights against the actions of law-enforcement agencies brought the Court into almost constant conflict with police, politicians, and the public.

A Look Forward

"Though the Supreme Court may decide a case," one political scientist has said, "it does not always settle an issue." This is certainly true of the search-and-seizure protections guaranteed by the Fourth Amendment. Many issues remain unsettled, and new ones will certainly develop in the future.

Daily papers and television broadcasts give us some idea of what might lie ahead. During 1990 alone, these stories made the news:

- St. Sabina Academy, a school in Chicago, began random drug testing of sixth- , seventh- , and eighth-grade students. This program was apparently the first in the nation to subject primary-school students to random drug testing. Are measures like these necessary to guard against drug abuse in the nation's education system? Or are they an unnecessary violation of students' Fourth Amendment rights?
- A Connecticut case involved a homeless man named David Mooney. He had been sentenced to prison for murder. Mooney appealed his conviction. Evidence used against him at his trial had been obtained from an area under a highway overpass where he had been living. The police had no search warrant. Therefore, Mooney claimed, he had been the victim of an unreasonable search and seizure. Can a public space be considered a "home" and so require a warrant for a legal search? Or is such a place beyond the protection of the Fourth Amendment?
- A pilot program in New York City public schools set up X-ray machines and metal detectors in efforts to reduce the number of weapons brought into school buildings. Other cities have taken similar steps. Are these measures needed to prevent school violence? Or are they an unnecessary violation of students' Fourth Amendment rights?

- Ade Adedokian, a Nigerian living in the United States legally, was detained for eight hours at the airport after returning to his home in Houston, Texas. Unfortunately, he fit a drug-courier profile that Drug Enforcement Administration agents rely on to catch smugglers. Must travelers submit to this sort of treatment for the public good? Or does it, as some people claim, target blacks unfairly?

- The Supreme Court ruled that the Fourth Amendment does not protect foreigners in foreign countries from warrantless searches and seizures conducted without a warrant by U.S. law-enforcement agents. Was this decision justified on the grounds that "the people" referred to in the Fourth Amendment does not mean "aliens outside of the United States territory"? (This is what the Supreme Court's majority opinion held.) Or was it an example of what a critic called "naked power" overwhelming the rule of the law?

In discussing what is meant by "the people," we return to the very first phrase of the Fourth Amendment, and to its heart. For the Fourth Amendment protects all the people, the guilty as well as the innocent. In fact, it has been said that the Fourth Amendment is almost always called on by those who are guilty of a crime. Justice Frankfurter expressed the idea in this way:

Freedom of speech, of the press, of religion, easily summon powerful support against encroachment [violation]. The prohibition against unreasonable search and seizure is normally invoked [called on] by those accused of crime, and criminals have few friends.

At first glance, statements like this may make us feel that the Fourth Amendment is a sort of necessary evil. Nothing could be further from the truth. We need to remember, as one writer put it, that "the rights of the best . . . will be observed only so long as the rights of the worst . . . are respected.'' We may never be in danger of having our homes unlawfully searched or our possessions illegally seized. But the existence of the Fourth Amendment and the procedures used to enforce it create a climate of fairness and justice for all.

Think back to the time when James Otis spoke out against British writs of assistance in Boston. In doing so, he wasn't attacking individual acts of oppression, such as the search of Daniel Malcom's house. What Otis objected to was a system of government that allowed its agents a free hand to invade the privacy of its citizens. Unlike the colonists of the 1760s, we have a shield, the Fourth Amendment, to protect us from the ''arbitrary power'' against which Otis warned.

$\mathscr{I}$MPORTANT $\mathscr{D}$ATES

1761 James Otis speaks out against writs of assistance.

1775–1783 United States wins independence from England after fighting American Revolution.

1789 Constitution is ratified.

1791 Fourth Amendment is adopted as part of the Bill of Rights.

1806 Supreme Court rules in *ex parte Burford*, first Fourth Amendment case.

1868 Fourteenth Amendment is ratified.

1886 Supreme Court decision in *Boyd* v. *United States* links Fourth and Fifth Amendments.

1914 In *Weeks* v. *United States*, Supreme Court establishes exclusionary rule for federal criminal trials.

1920–1933 National Prohibition is in effect.

1925 In *Carroll* v. *United States*, Supreme Court allows warrantless searches for "automobile exception."

1927 In *Marron* v. *United States*, Supreme Court allows warrantless searches incidental to arrest.

1928 Supreme Court rules, in *Olmstead* v. *United States*, that wiretap evidence is legal.

1934 Federal Communications Act tries to limit use of wiretapping.

1949 Supreme Court decision in *Wolf* v. *Colorado* incorporates Fourth Amendment into Fourteenth.

1952 Supreme Court limits invasive body searches in *Rochin* v. *California*.

1961 Supreme Court, in *Mapp* v. *Ohio*, extends exclusionary rule to state criminal trials.

1967 Decision by Supreme Court in *Katz* v. *United States* holds that Fourth Amendment protects spoken communication. Harlan sets forth "expectation of privacy" standard.

1968 Omnibus Crime Control and Safe Streets Act gives government broad wiretapping authority.

1968 Supreme Court decision in *Terry* v. *Ohio* sets reasonableness standard for certain stop-and-frisk cases.

1969 In *Chimel* v. *California* decision, Supreme Court limits premises that can be searched without a warrant.

1971 Supreme Court decision in *Bivens* case allows damage suits against federal officials. Burger opinion criticizes exclusionary rule.

1972 In case of *Adams* v. *Williams,* Supreme Court allows car searches based on tip by reliable informant.

1973 Supreme Court limits border searches in *Almeida-Sanchez* v. *United States.*

1984 In *United States* v. *Leon* decision, Supreme Court sets "good faith" standard for search warrants.

1985 In *New Jersey* v. *T.L.O.,* Supreme Court approves warrantless search of student by school officials.

1986 Supreme Court rules aerial searches legal in *California* v. *Ciraolo.*

1988 Supreme Court, in *California* v. *Greenwood* decision, declares expectation of privacy does not apply to garbage.

1989 Government begins Zero Tolerance Program to aid drug searches at sea.

1989 Supreme Court decision in *United States* v. *Sokolow* approves use of drug-courier profile.

1989 In two decisions, Supreme Court allows drug testing for railroad and Customs Service employees.

1990 In *Alabama* v. *White,* Supreme Court allows automobile search based on tip by anonymous informant.

1990 Supreme Court decision in *James* v. *Illinois* reaffirms exclusionary rule.

$\mathscr{G}$LOSSARY

alien   A resident of a country who is not a citizen.

amendment   A change in the Constitution.

appeal   To refer a case to a higher court so that it will review the decision of a lower court.

automobile exception   An exception to the Fourth Amendment requirement for a search warrant. It allows the police, if they have probable cause, to stop and search a moving vehicle.

bail   Money paid by the accused to gain his or her release in the period before trial to make sure he or she will show up for the trial. If the accused does not appear, he or she loses the money.

bill of attainder   A law pronouncing a person guilty of a serious crime without a trial.

civil case   A law case in which private individuals or businesses sue each other over property or money.

common law   Law based not on acts passed by lawmaking bodies but rather on customs, traditions, and court decisions.

concurring opinion   An opinion by one or more judges that agrees with the majority opinion but offers different reasons for reaching the decision.

criminal case   A law case involving a crime against society (such as robbery or murder), punished by the government.

customs   Taxes imposed by a government on goods brought into or sent out of a country.

dissenting opinion   An opinion by one or more judges that disagrees with the majority opinion.

double jeopardy   Putting a person on trial for a crime for which he or she has already been tried.

exclusionary rule   A rule, based on Fourth Amendment protections, which holds that illegally obtained evidence cannot be used in a criminal trial.

executive branch   The branch or part of the government that carries out the laws and makes sure they are obeyed.

ex post facto **law**   A law that makes illegal an action that took place before the law was passed.

federalism   The system by which the states and the federal government each has certain special powers and shares others.

general warrant   An arrest or search warrant that does not specify the person to be arrested or the property to be seized.

habeas corpus   The right of someone who has been arrested to be brought into court and formally charged.

hot pursuit exception   An exception to the Fourth Amendment requirement for a search warrant. It allows a warrantless search of premises if police have pursued someone there whom they suspect of having committed a serious crime.

incorporation   The process of making Bill of Rights protections apply to the states so that people are safeguarded against state actions violating these rights.

indictment   A grand jury's written accusation that the person named has committed a crime.

judicial activism   A trend among courts or judges to expand their powers by making policy.

judicial branch   The part or branch of the government that interprets the laws.

judicial restraint   The belief that judges should have great respect for legislatures and executives, overruling their actions only when such actions are clearly unconstitutional.

judicial review   The power of the courts to review the decisions of other parts or levels of the government. A court may review the decision of a lower court and come to a different decision.

legislative branch   The part or branch of the government that makes the laws.

majority opinion   The statement of a court's decision in which the majority of its members join.

plain view exception   An exception to the Fourth Amendment requirement for a search warrant. It allows the police to make a warrantless seizure if, while legally on premises, they spot something incriminating.

precedent   A court decision that guides future decisions.

premises   Buildings or parts of buildings and the land around them.

probable cause   A reasonable belief that the objects of a search or seizure are in a given place or that a person should be arrested.

profile   A list of characteristics and behaviors that are thought to be typical of a certain kind of a person, such as a drug smuggler.

ratification   Approval of an amendment to the Constitution by three-fourths of state legislatures or conventions (after the amendment has been officially proposed by two-thirds of each house of Congress or proposed by a convention called by two-thirds of the states).

separation of powers   The division of the government into three parts or branches—the legislative, the executive, and the judicial.

stop and frisk   A situation in which police officers who are suspicious of someone stop the person and run their hands lightly over the suspect's outer clothes to see whether he or she is carrying a concealed weapon.

warrant   A written document issued by a government official that gives an officer the power to carry out an arrest, search, seizure, or other action.

writ of assistance   A written document issued by a government official allowing an officer to conduct an almost unlimited search and seizure and to ask for help in doing so.

$\mathscr{S}$UGGESTED $\mathscr{R}$EADING

Abraham, Henry J. *Freedom and the Court.* New York: Oxford University Press, 1988.

Amsterdam, Anthony. *Perspectives on the Fourth Amendment.* Minneapolis: Minnesota Law Review, 1974.

Barker, Lucius J., and Twiley W. Barker, Jr. *Civil Liberties and the Constitution.* Englewood Cliffs, N.J.: Prentice-Hall, 1986.

Barth, Allen. *The Rights of Free Men.* New York: Alfred A. Knopf, 1984.

The Bill of Rights and Beyond: A Resource Guide. The Commission on the Bicentennial of the United States Constitution, 1990.

Bickel, Alexander M. *The Supreme Court and the Idea of Progress.* New York: Harper & Row, 1970.

Blasi, Vincent, ed. *The Burger Court.* New Haven: Yale University Press, 1983.

Corwin, Edward S. *The Constitution and What It Means Today.* Princeton: Princeton University Press, 1978.

Federal Government Information Technology: Electronic Surveillance and Civil Liberties. Washington, D.C.: U.S. Government Printing Office, 1985.

*Friendly, Fred, and Martha Elliott. *The Constitution.* New York: Random House, 1984.

Graham, Fred P. *The Self-Inflicted Wound.* New York: Macmillan, 1970.

Hirschel, J. D. *Fourth Amendment Rights.* Lexington, Mass.: Lexington Books, 1979.

*Hoobler, Dorothy, and Thomas Hoobler. *Your Right to Privacy.* New York: Franklin Watts, 1986.

Kelly, Alfred H., and Winfred Harbison. *The American Constitution.* New York: W.W. Norton, 1990.

*Konvitz, Milton. *The Bill of Rights Reader.* Ithaca: Cornell University Press, 1973.

Landynski, J. W. *Search and Seizure and the Supreme Court.* Baltimore: Johns Hopkins University Press, 1966.

Lapidus, Edith J. *Eavesdropping on Trial.* Indianapolis: Hayden Books, 1974.

Lasson, Nelson B. *The History and Development of the Fourth Amendment to the United States Constitution.* Baltimore: Johns Hopkins University Press, 1937.

Levy, Leonard. *Against the Law.* New York: Harper & Row, 1974.

*Lieberman, Jethro K. *The Enduring Constitution.* St. Paul, Minn.: West, 1987.

*Peck, Robert S. *We the People.* New York: Harry N. Abrams, 1987.

Rutland, Robert. *The Birth of the Bill of Rights.* Chapel Hill: University of North Carolina Press, 1955.

Schwartz, Bernard. *The Great Rights of Mankind.* New York: Oxford University Press, 1977.

Uviller, H. Richard. *Tempered Zeal.* Chicago: Contemporary Books, 1988.

Wilson, Bradford P. *Enforcing the Fourth Amendment: A Jurisprudential History.* New York: Garland, 1986.

Wise, David. *The American Police State.* New York: Vintage Books, 1976.

*Readers of *The Fourth Amendment* by Paula A. Franklin will find these books particularly readable.

$\mathscr{S}$OURCES

Abraham, Henry J. *Freedom and the Court.* New York: Oxford University Press, 1988.

Adams, John. *Works.* Edited by Albert B. Hart. In *American History Told by Contemporaries.* New York: Macmillan, 1893.

Albanese, Jay S. *Justice, Privacy, and Crime Control.* Lanham, Md.: University Press of America, 1984.

Amsterdam, Anthony. *Perspectives on the Fourth Amendment.* Minneapolis: Minnesota Law Review, 1974.

Barker, Lucius J., and Twiley W. Barker, Jr. *Civil Liberties and the Constitution.* Englewood Cliffs, N.J.: Prentice-Hall, 1986.

Blasi, Vincent, ed. *The Burger Court.* New Haven: Yale University Press, 1983.

Corwin, Edward S. *The Constitution and What It Means Today.* Princeton: Princeton University Press, 1978.

Edwards, Richard. *The Effect of an Unreasonable Search and Seizure.* Ph.D. dissertation. Columbia University, 1952.

Falco, Mathea. *Winning the Drug War.* New York: Priority Press, 1989.

Federal Government Information Technology: Electronic Surveillance and Civil Liberties. Washington, D.C.: U.S. Government Printing Office, 1985.

Gardner, Martin R. "Student Privacy in the Wake of *T.L.O.:* An Appeal for an Individualized Suspicion Requirement for Valid Searches and Seizures in the Schools." *Georgia Law Review* (Summer 1988), pp. 897–947.

Garrow, David J. *The FBI and Martin Luther King, Jr.* New York: W.W. Norton, 1981.

Gildea, Andrew J., and David J. Weiler. "Unreasonable Searches and Seizures." *American Criminal Law Review* (Spring 1989), pp. 1397–1432.

Graham, Fred P. *The Self-Inflicted Wound.* New York: Macmillan, 1970.

Hall, John Wesley, Jr. *Search and Seizure.* Rochester, N.Y.: Lawyers Co-Operative, 1982.

———. *Cumulative Supplement*, 1988.

Harwood, Edwin. *In Liberty's Shadow.* Stanford: Hoover Institution Press, 1986.

Hull, Elizabeth. *Without Justice for All.* Westport, Conn.: Greenwood Press, 1985.

Kobler, John. *Ardent Spirits.* New York: G.P. Putnam's Sons, 1973.

Kyvig, David E., ed. *Law, Alcohol, and Order.* Westport, Conn.: Greenwood Press, 1985.

La Fave, Wayne R. *Search and Seizure.* St. Paul, Minn.: West, 1978.

Landynski, J. W. *Search and Seizure and the Supreme Court.* Baltimore: Johns Hopkins University Press, 1966.

Lapidus, Edith J. *Eavesdropping on Trial.* Indianapolis: Hayden Books, 1974.

Lasson, Nelson B. *The History and Development of the Fourth Amendment to the United States Constitution.* Baltimore: Johns Hopkins University Press, 1937.

Levy, Leonard. *Against the Law.* New York: Harper & Row, 1974.

Oates, Stephen B. *Let the Trumpet Sound.* New York: Harper & Row, 1982.

Quick, Albert T. "The School Administrator's Guide to Search and Seizure," *Journal of Law and Education* (July 1985), pp. 409–419.

"Report to the Attorney General on the Search and Seizure Exclusionary Rule." *University of Michigan Journal of Law Reform* (Spring/Summer 1989), pp. 573–659.

Richardson, James F. *The New York Police.* New York: Oxford University Press, 1970.

Ringel, William E. *Searches and Seizures, Arrests and Confessions.* New York: Clark Boardman, 1990.

Rutland, Robert. *The Birth of the Bill of Rights.* Chapel Hill: University of North Carolina Press, 1955.

Schwartz, Bernard. *The Great Rights of Mankind.* New York: Oxford University Press, 1977.

Smith, M. H. *The Writs of Assistance Case.* Berkeley: University of California Press, 1978.

Tocqueville, Alexis de. *Democracy in America.* New York: Vintage Books, 1945.

To the Promised Land. New York: Aperture Foundation, 1988.

Uviller, H. Richard. *Tempered Zeal.* Chicago: Contemporary Books, 1988.

Wasserstrom, Silas J. "The Fourth Amendment's Two Clauses," *American Criminal Law Review* (Spring 1989), pp. 1389–1396.

Wolkins, George G. "Daniel Malcom and Writs of Assistance." Massachusetts Historical Society *Proceedings* (October 1924–June 1925), pp. 5–84.

$\mathcal{I}$NDEX OF CASES

Paula A. Franklin was born in Springfield, Illinois, and lives in New York City. She is coauthor of two United States history texts and the author of *Our Nation's Constitution*. Her hobby is choral singing.

Warren E. Burger was Chief Justice of the United States from 1969 to 1986. Since 1985 he has served as chairman of the Commission on the Bicentennial of the United States Constitution. He is also chancellor of the College of William and Mary, Williamsburg, Virginia; chancellor emeritus of the Smithsonian Institution; and a life trustee of the National Geographic Society. Prior to his appointment to the Supreme Court, Chief Justice Burger was Assistant Attorney General of the United States (Civil Division) and judge of the United States Court of Appeals, District of Columbia Circuit.

Philip A. Klinkner graduated from Lake Forest College in 1985 and is now finishing his Ph.D. in political science at Yale University. He is currently a Governmental Studies Fellow at the Brookings Institution in Washington, D.C. Klinkner is the author of *The First Amendment* and *The Ninth Amendment* in *The American Heritage History of the Bill of Rights*.